Teacner's Tackle Box

Sue Nothstine
Nancy Piercy
Dr. Joyce Piveral

Copyright © 2009, 2017 by Sue Nothstine, Nancy Piercy and Dr. Joyce Piveral.

All rights reserved. No part of this publication may be reproduced, stored in a retrieval system or transmitted, in any form, or by any means, electronic, mechanical, recorded, photocopied, or otherwise, without the prior permission of the copyright owner, except by a reviewer who may quote brief passages in a review.

Printed in the United States of America

ISBN: 978-1945667367

Dedication

This book is dedicated to all the students and teachers we have known and loved throughout the years. You have taught us so much and inspired us to share. May our work support many future superior teachers.

Acknowledgments

This project could not have been completed without encouragement from our families, friends, and students. Thank you to our respective husbands for their ongoing support, both emotional and financial. We specifically appreciate Don Nothstine, for his marketing knowledge, Dan Piercy, for his accounting and tax expertise and Don Piveral for his teaching experience and his no-nonsense attitude. Thank you to Joann Anderson, Bob Bartlett, Pat Burton, Dr. Max Fridell, Joann Olson, Myra Reisinger, Jean Shearer, and Danyell Wiederholt who read early chapters of the book and gave us insight and direction. Thank you to Nancy Archer, Bill Baldwin, Charlotte Basinger, Renee Beggs, Sally Bryan, Carol Conard, Barbara Denton, Matt Hoskins, Eva Morlock, Dot Nelson, Ruth Newhart, Don Piveral, Roger Price, Betty Schieber, Carol Scoglund, Marcia Steeby, Danyell Wiederholt, and Lori Zillner who have opened their treasure chests and inspired us with their golden moments and snapshot memories. Thank you to all of our students, over the years, for sharing their lives with us and teaching us so much. Special thanks go to Joshua Cotter, our illustrator, who brought humor and life to the pages. Thanks also to Amazing Things Press for their help and support with publishing this book.

Contents

Introduction	9	
Chapter One	Diving into Teaching – First Day	14
Chapter Two	Hook, Line, and Sinker - Communication	27
Chapter Three	Fishing for Success – Class Environment	43
Chapter Four	Hooking Students – Learning Styles	...55
Chapter Five	Gone Fishin' - Curriculum and Activities	66
Chapter Six	Celebrate Fish Diversity	80
Chapter Seven	Sink or Swim – Classroom Management	98
Chapter Eight	Casting for Positive Parents	115
Chapter Nine	Gasping for Air - Dealing with Stress	..127
Chapter Ten	Angling for a Career	138
Final Thoughts	149	
The T.Box…Our Gift to You…Free	151	
References	153	
Index	155	

Introduction

Congratulations! You are a teacher!

You have chosen one of the most rewarding, exciting, and demanding professions. You have selected a career in which you will have the opportunity to become a positive influence in the lives of hundreds of young people.

 **Golden Moment**

A veteran second-grade teacher was enjoying the state teachers' conference. Shortly after a session, a young woman smiled warmly and greeted her by name. The woman explained, "I was in your second-grade class years ago. I want you to know you are the reason I am a teacher today. You were so inspiring!"

As a teacher, you will have the opportunity to positively influence the lives of hundreds, maybe even thousands of young people. You will experience the joy of opening the windows of the world to your students. You will empower them with knowledge and inspire them with your compassion, love and respect. You will stimulate their creativity and stir their imagination. And when you are ready to hang up your trusty colored pen or your smiley-faced stickers, the rewards will continue to come your way in the form of priceless golden moments. You have been on the other side of the teacher's desk since you were five or six years old. Now the classroom is yours. Don't panic!

You can do the job, and you can do it well. You have all those years of education behind you. In addition, you have in your hands our legacy to you. This easy-to-read, how-to book will tell you almost everything you need to know. We have combined our knowledge, skills, and experiences from one-hundred-plus years of teaching to assist you in becoming a superior teacher.

> *"He who dares to teach must never cease to learn."*
> — *Richard Henry Dann*

Go ahead, thumb through the book. See … it is not a textbook. The first things you probably notice are the humorous fish cartoons, the thought-provoking reflective pools, and the reference information and ideas you can access from going to our website and downloading the free resources from our T.Box. We have used the fish theme throughout the book to unify the information and to have some fun. So suspend your cynicism, relax, and enjoy this helpful book. Read the golden moments shared by veteran teachers, identify with the personal snapshots, and try your hand at the exercises. You will be surprised at the useful things you learn.

Now, glance through the table of contents; the chapters focus on solutions for real problems that happen in the classroom and in the school environment. We've provided helpful tips to guide you through those first few hectic days. You'll learn how to maintain a positive learning environment when you have many students who are eager to learn and others who are disruptive. We share advice on how to talk to parents even if you have to tell them their child is not always a model student. There are also suggestions to help you deal with that student who is sleeping in your class and with the flirtatious teenager who has a crush on you. There is information to help you decide when you have done all that you can and must enlist the help of others. We offer many ideas to help invigorate your classroom and to keep you and your kids energized. We have even included ideas to help you take care of yourself and maintain your love of teaching and sense of humor.

As a teacher, you will be remembered for the knowledge you impart and the compassion you share. You will create valuable memories for your students because you will make a positive difference in their lives. In return, you will be rewarded with many unexpected golden moments throughout your career. This is the real currency paid to teachers and what keeps them coming back to the classroom year after year. Throughout this book, you will be treated to many golden moments.

 **Golden Moment**

An eighty-five-year-old, retired schoolteacher sat on her front porch watching the yellow highway machinery move back and forth, expanding the two-lane highway bordering her farm. She was surprised when one of the tall workmen in his yellow hardhat came walking up the hill toward the house.

"Weren't you a teacher?"

"Yes," she replied.

With that, the workman enveloped the little lady in his arms with a big hug, nearly swinging her off her feet. He set her down and stepped back, saying the golden words, "Don't you know me?"

The man then recounted his first day of school. His mother had made him wear short pants, and the other children were teasing him unmercifully. The teacher stood him up straight, wiped off his tear-stained face, and said, "Why, I believe you have lovely little legs. These are fine legs. Ignore the others; we'll have a good time at school today." She made sure he did enjoy school that day, and he never forgot her for that simple kindness. This teacher, long after her teaching days were over, was still being paid in "golden moment currency."

Don't ever underestimate your influence. Look at all those young faces in front of you. Your students are watching you, listening to you and scrutinizing your words. Think about it. Most of those students sitting in your room will probably spend more time with their teachers during the next nine months than they will spend with any other adults. They expect you to teach them, guide them, inspire them, and love them.

> *"As a general rule, teachers teach more by what they are than by what they say."* — Anonymous

Feeling a bit overwhelmed? Don't flip out of the fishbowl! You can do it. We know that you won't see all this in the fine print when you sign your contract, but that is the beauty of this job. You get to do it all. By the end of the year, you will have become a nurse, parent, counselor, police officer, friend, social worker, janitor, loan officer, bouncer, entertainer, mediator, hero, coach, politician, and, oh yes, a great teacher. You will become that one special teacher who will inspire others to follow their dreams and realize their unique potentials.

Golden Moment

The girls loved Penny, their physical education teacher and volleyball coach. They often confided in her, and some became very close with her because she facilitated weekly support groups for students whose parents were involved with drugs and/or alcohol. One day when Penny came into the office before school to pick up her mail, Jackie, a senior, was standing at the counter filling out some paperwork. When Penny asked what she was doing, Jackie said that she was dropping out of school.

Penny was shocked because there were only four more weeks of school, and Jackie had been a decent student. Jackie said that she had missed a lot of school that semester and just wasn't in the mood to finish. Penny convinced Jackie that day that she would graduate if she could just come for the last four weeks. Several years later, Jackie and Penny saw each other in a shopping mall. Jackie told Penny that if they hadn't talked that day, she would have dropped out and probably wouldn't have graduated.

We hope this book is a lifesaver that will keep you hooked on teaching and angling with the best. Peruse it, use it, and abuse it. Feel free to highlight passages and write in the margins and open spaces. Reflect, reject, or embrace the ideas we bring to you. Welcome to our world. May your teaching treasure chest be filled with many golden moments.

Chapter One
Diving into Teaching

Key Topics:

- **Navigating Uncharted Waters**
- **Anticipation**
- **Reality Bites!**

Navigating Uncharted Waters

The few days before your first day of teaching seem like an endless procession of meetings. First, you attend the new teachers' welcome and orientation meeting. You find that you look and act very much like other fish in the bowl. At the meeting, you are reminded you are considered a BT, so you probably need some PD or BTAP. This has been discerned because DESE says you will be assessed by the PBTE and PCL. Sorry you can't avoid those pesky acronyms. The experienced teacher knows these language shortcuts, but they can make you feel isolated and ill at ease if they are unfamiliar.

(By-the-way, BT = Beginning Teacher, PD = Professional Development, DESE = Department of Elementary and Secondary Education, PBTE = Performance-Based Teacher Evaluation, PCL = Professional Certification Level, and BTAP = Beginning Teacher Assistance Program.)

TIP: *During meetings, jot down acronyms you do not know. Make friends with a veteran teacher and have him/her explain what each one stands for and what it represents. Knowing the language is the first step to joining the new culture at your school. It will assist you in becoming an insider.*

The next meeting is building wide. Here, the crowd is much larger, and variety abounds. You feel like a small fish in a big, crowded bowl. You notice an angelfish in high heels with a Jimmy Choo purse (how can she afford that on a teacher's salary?), sweaty muskies in shorts, carrying whistles, and a distracted one-lined  pencil fish in a lab coat who wandered in half an hour late. They are laughing and visiting and seem so comfortable with one another.

You no longer look and act like everyone else. You feel like you have a sign around your neck reading, "bottom feeder," and you feel left out. At this meeting, the building principal talks about a variety of topics: committees, extracurricular activities, fundraising, class sizes, textbooks, missing desks, and parking arrangements. The principal then introduces new faculty and staff. You stand to a smattering of applause. You are embarrassed.

You discover you must buy a parking card from someone, but you miss his name; consequently, you'll have to park across campus  again tomorrow and walk a maze of hallways to get to your classroom. Also, you've been assigned as a junior-class sponsor (you hate proms). Finally, you must report to the computer lab after this meeting for training in how to take roll and keep grades. Don't hyperventilate … take a deep breath and relax. Remember, next year you'll be in the swim.

Diving into Teaching

TIP: *There is no real way to soften the shock of this initial meeting except to recognize that it will occur and that you will survive. Don't be shy. Question the person next to you when you don't understand something. Better yet, if you have been given a mentor, sit with that mentor; he/she will help you. If asking questions immediately is not possible, make notes about what is unclear so you can figure it out later.*

You find your way to the computer lab by following the other teachers. The training is what you expected. You follow the step-by-step procedure to find your class rolls. You notice you have forty students enrolled in one class. Do you have that many chairs? (Don't fish die when the fishbowl becomes overcrowded?) You are taught how to take roll and are introduced to the computer grade book. Everyone seems to understand—everyone but you. You know full well that when you sit down by yourself at your own computer, none of this will work. Be patient.

> *"All you need to be a fisherman is patience and a worm."* —Herb Shriner

TIP: *First, recognize that most of those other new teachers do not understand any better than you. They are just treading water and trying to stay afloat. Get together with another new teacher to work with the software. If you cannot figure out the system, find a veteran teacher to ask for help. Keep looking until you find the right teacher. Be assured, there are certain teachers in the building who excel with technology and love to initiate new folks. After all, they are teachers.*

The next morning, you face department meetings. (If you are at a very small school, you may be the department, in which case, you do not have to meet with yourself.) Relax: you will be working closely with this much smaller group and can depend on these people. Assume your chairperson is a rockfish, not a crab, even though he/she informs you that your textbooks will not be in for another two weeks. Try not to panic about that class of forty students; you will be told, "things will even out eventually."

Speak up. This is the time and place for your unanswered questions from yesterday. Here, you should notice camaraderie and cohesion, which might not have been as evident in the building meeting. Remember, department loyalty and working with your team will be rewarding.

"Don't wait for your ship to come in; swim out to it." —Anonymous

TIP: Look for the department member who seems most helpful and knowledgeable about your questions. Do not be afraid to ask for help or to appear that you do not know what to do in difficult situations. You won't know all the answers at first. The others have been through the same thing. They will understand. Ask questions about class size and supplies. Find out who teaches classes similar to yours, get their room numbers, and use them as resources. Have a coworker show you where the nearest copier and copy paper are located and what to do when the machine is jammed. Usually, one of the nearby teachers or a janitor can coax the machine into working order, if you know whom to call. Find out where the teachers' workroom is located; there might be a restroom there.

That afternoon, you get to spend time preparing your classroom. You remember that the textbooks on which you have based some of the first week's lesson plans will not be in for another two weeks. You may need to rework those instructional plans. Oh well, you can think about that tonight.

You arrange the student seating and line up paper and pencils on the teacher's desk. Now you need to go to the office to get your own set of keys and classroom supplies. You try to get the route to the office clearly in mind.

> *TIP: Get to know the secretaries and janitors right away, and be very nice to them, even if at first they might appear to be barracudas. They can help you so much. They know all the secrets, and the school cannot run without them.*

On the way back to your classroom, you reflect on the complicated directions for taking attendance. You have just endured a short course from the attendance secretary about the importance of keeping these records accurately, and you don't want to be snarled in her fishing line. As you start thinking about tomorrow, when the students will arrive, you get excited. You have spent a great deal of time preparing for this. You have wanted to be a teacher since Mr. Smart gave you a love of learning and inspired you in his classroom. Now, it is your turn to pass that love and inspiration on to your students.

> *TIP: Look over the class rolls, and be sure you can pronounce your students' names. Plan to work at learning your students' names and faces so you can recognize them as soon as possible. This is very important. Carrying a seating chart with you for the first week is a big help. Do an introductory*

activity in which you can learn some bit of personal information from each student (See T.Box: Start-up Activities). Get that information in writing so you can review it that night and greet students individually the next day. Personal connections are keys to displaying genuine interest in and a caring attitude toward students.

> *"People will not care what you know until they know how much you care." —Anonymous*

It is time to go home and plan for the students' first day. You spend most of the evening revising lessons plans that were based on the missing textbooks. You choose with care one new outfit that will help you feel good and professional the first day.

TIP: Check out the norms for teacher dress in your building. Do not dress like the kids. Leave your faded jeans on the bedroom floor, and cover up any inappropriate tattoos. You need to establish a difference between yourself and the students. You are not going to be their peer; you are going to teach them. Expect their respect, even though you will have to work hard to gain it. Your appearance is an important beginning.

You want to arrive an hour before the students so you can have everything in place. That will give you time to create a projection slide, to photocopy some handouts (hope the copier is working), and to check on the lunch schedule again. Finally, you are ready for a restful night's sleep before that oh-so-important first day.

Anticipation

Remember the childlike anticipation you felt each year when it was almost time for school to start? For a week or two before the school year began, you went shopping for new pencils, ink pens, notebooks (college ruled for Mrs. Neat, the American history teacher), scissors, and colored pencils (for those geography maps). You also added some of the latest clothing fashions so you could fit in with your peers. The night before the first day of school, you were unable to sleep because you were doing an imaginary run-through of the day.

Well, this year is not so different, although you are the one in charge. You are the teacher. Your tackle box is full of the latest supplies: stickers, paper clips, pencils, ink pens (be sure to include some colored ones; you get to grade those papers now), scissors, rulers, construction paper, and colored pencils. You want to be well prepared for the future doctors, plumbers, nurses, teachers, business leaders, factory workers, presidents, barbers, mothers, fathers, and others facing you the next day.

> *"Teaching is the essential profession, the one that makes all professions possible." —David Haselkorn*

Set the alarm, and settle into bed for a restful night. At least, that is the plan. Again, you lay awake the night before school, unable to sleep because you are doing the imaginary run-through of the first day. After an hour of tossing and turning, you have thought of every imaginable happening and what you would do to save the day. Okay, look at the clock; it is 1:00 AM, and you need to be up at 5:30 to take a shower and get to school by 7:00. Still, sleep eludes you as you toss and turn in anticipation of the most exciting day of the school year.

Your alarm buzzes. That day is finally here! You eat and dress quickly, eager to start your career as a teacher. You are the kingfish. As you drive to school, you think of the power and control you will have now:

- ❖ You won't have to raise your hand to ask if you can go to the bathroom.
- ❖ You will have no homework to hand in.
- ❖ You won't have to go anywhere single file.
- ❖ Recess and a planning period mean relaxation time.
- ❖ You will get the adult portion (six) instead of the student portion (four) of chicken nuggets for lunch.
- ❖ You will have your own classroom with your own computer to assist with record keeping.
- ❖ You will be in control; the students will do what you say.
- ❖ The room will fall silent when you say, "Quiet!"

Reality Bites!

The long-anticipated morning has arrived, and you head to your classroom armed with the "Classroom of Dreams" philosophy from practicum class:

If I teach, they will learn.

In that tackle box of teacher tricks, you have the "Burger King" classroom-management plan:

I will have it my way.

You anxiously await the arrival of students eager to learn. As they come through your door, most are talking and laughing boisterously, although a few seem shy and almost fearful. Some are sporting the latest fashions, while others wear faded jeans with torn-out knees and oversized T-shirts. Many girls have small, tight tops with thin straps and low-waist shorts or slacks. How are you going to be able to hook all students (especially the boys) with this competition for classroom focus? You become more than a little worried about a young man who has on a pair of long shorts that are barely hanging on, exposing a great deal of his colorful boxers. You question if this is in line with the dress code for students, which was described in the teacher handbook you hardly had time to look through during new teacher orientation. (Where did you put that thing?) You are not sure you want to start your day—no, your year—with a confrontation about dress.

> *TIP: Don't start with confrontation. On your first day, you must establish a good rapport with the students and begin to gain their trust. Once they find they like and respect you, you can set them straight in many ways, and they will accept it. Until then, you will simply alienate them. Do not openly react to the kid with pierced eyebrows and purple hair. Unless the manner of dress is totally out of line, let the issue lie. Also, keep in mind this is the first day of school, and the office is very busy; adding your student to the office chaos may not be the best solution to your problem.*

It is now time to begin class. You start by calling roll, working hard to become familiar with the students' names and faces, and you report the attendance via the computer. (Remember, if you don't do it right the first time, you won't be the only one.) Suddenly, you hear noise and static coming from a corner of the room. You realize it is the public address system, which has been turned on for the daily announcements. You forgot to plan for this. How do you get the class to settle down and listen? You decide to take charge and tell the students that in your classroom the expectation is that everyone is quiet during the announcements.

TIP: *You must model your expectations. Therefore, during announcements you should be quiet and listen. Do not attempt to take attendance or do paperwork. Do not visit with individual students. Save classroom problems until later. This will emphasize to the class the importance of listening. It will assist you and them in finding out what is going on in the school building and when activities are being held. Let students know you will allow them some unstructured time to address student needs at the end of class, so they should be quiet now.*

> *"What you do speaks so loud that I cannot hear what you say."*
> *—Ralph Waldo Emerson*

Things go well. After announcements, the class interacts appropriately in the group activity you had planned. They listen quietly as you explain what they will be learning, your philosophy of education, and how the class work will be organized. They accept the first short assignment and turn in their papers without too much prodding. They seem appreciative when you tell them what is going to happen during the day.

TIP: *Find out if anyone has any questions. It is important to honor your students' questions as much as their answers. If anyone is new to the school and does not know his/her way around, get a volunteer buddy to accompany the student. You will win the hearts of those shy, struggling students with this simple kindness.*

You have ended your first day of teaching and are more exhausted than you had thought possible. However, you have made it through the day and have had many successes. You recognized students who were eager to learn, and you think you can affect their lives. You also recognized a few troubled students and vow to reach out to them with understanding and compassion.

As you reflect on this day, you again smile and think of the power and control you now have as a teacher:

- ❖ You would have loved to be able to raise your hand and go to the bathroom. (The only time you were free was during your planning period, and then you were rushed. You used most of that time in the office clearing up mistakes made on the attendance report.)
- ❖ You would rather do homework than grade numerous homework papers tonight.
- ❖ Going single file with an organized group would be welcome after trying to negotiate crowded halls.
- ❖ The planning period flew by without time to do any planning. You will need to do the planning tonight after you finish grading the papers.
- ❖ Any number of chicken nuggets would have been good. The lunch line was so long that you made it to the lunch table with only nine minutes left to eat.
- ❖ Unexpectedly, another teacher uses your classroom during your planning period so you cannot get to materials or your computer.
- ❖ The idea that others will follow directions and do as you say only worked part of the time. It is not like during student teaching, when the cooperating teacher was in the room or nearby and that was enough to back up your words.

❖ Quiet only comes when you are in the room approximately one hour after school with the door closed.

The Reflection Pool

Make some notes about your impressions of the start of school: What was a silly thing said or done at a meeting that you promise never to do? How did it feel to be a teacher in the building? What might you do differently next year in preparation for opening day?

Chapter Two

Hook, Line, and Sinker

Key Topics:

- **Communication Is your Hook**
- **Fishy Fundamentals**
- **Becoming a Multilingual Mimic Fish**

Communication Is Your Hook

Imagine being able to snorkel through your school building, swimming through the hallways above the classrooms and offices. You can clearly see the multilayered complexity of your new school. As you come to know staff members in the building, you are able to identify the sharks and the crocodiles. You see the fish that hang together in schools, as well as those who prefer to swim alone. You become aware of how difficult navigating the waters will be and how you will need to learn to have lunch with—and not become lunch for—some of the inhabitants.

So, what is the one essential skill to have in order to maneuver the ever-changing waters that flow through your school? What is your job all about? Is it possible to identify one essential survival skill? Yes, it is. Simply stated, it is communication.

You were hired to teach, and teaching primarily involves communicating ideas and building relationships with the students, teachers, parents, administrators, and staff. Your survival as a teacher is affected by how well you communicate.

You've been communicating verbally and nonverbally since the day you were born. What could be so tough about communication? The big deal is knowing how to communicate your thoughts and feelings so the recipient understands them. You have to know how to adjust your verbal and nonverbal communication so you can engage others.

Your nonverbal cues—the expression on your face, the tone in your voice, the way you stand and posture your body—send messages about how you feel. If you have your hands on your hips, a snarl on your face, and sarcasm in your voice while you are saying "I'm sorry," then your apology probably won't be accepted. Your nonverbal and verbal cues must match if you want your message understood.

To become an effective communicator, you must understand people—how they think, what they feel, and what does and doesn't motivate them. You need to share ideas and feelings without antagonizing your listener. Even constructive criticism—if direct, heartfelt, and given with a positive stroke—can be well received.

Golden Moment

A former student stopped an experienced teacher on the street one day, going out of his way to shake her hand. "I want to thank you. Something you said specifically to me in our science class many years ago has really helped to shape my future. Thank you so much!"

The teacher felt very pleased and naturally inquired, "What did I say that made such a difference to you?"

He promptly replied, "You told me I was one of the brightest young men you had ever had in class, and one of the laziest. You let me know, if I continued in that manner, I would never make it in college. I really thought about what you said. I have since completed a degree in business, and I am now in medical school."

You should be a student of human behavior, someone who is flexible and adaptable in most verbal transactions. Being able to read people and respond appropriately are necessary when building relationships.

Initial communications are important. Be sure to communicate what you mean. When you walk into a new school building, you are at a disadvantage because most people already have navigated the waters and know where the crocodiles, sharks, blowfish, clownfish, triggerfish, and turtles live. They have learned through experience how to approach different faculty members, how to negotiate with the principal, and how to talk to the most difficult student.

As you walk along the shore, you wonder, "Where do I jump into the water and begin?" Maybe the first thing to do is to review a couple of simple but effective communication skills. One useful communication skill uses "I" messages. If you need to talk directly to someone about a misunderstanding, consider using an "I" statement instead of a "you" statement.

Use the following format for "I" messages:

I feel_____

when you_____

because_____

and I want you to_____.

Here is an example to illustrate the difference between an effective "I" message and an antagonizing "you" message:

 ## Teacher Snapshot

One day, it became necessary to ask the weightlifters across the hall from our classroom to turn down the volume on their music. We could have stormed across the hall and said, "Do you realize that there are people in this building trying to actually learn and make a future for themselves? What makes you think you can blast your music as loud as you want? Don't you ever think of anyone besides yourselves?" Instead, one of us approached them by saying, "You know, <u>I feel</u> frustrated <u>when</u> your music is so loud <u>because</u> I am unable to do my job effectively. <u>I want you to</u> turn the volume down so my students and I can't hear it. Would you please do that for me? Thank you."

Do you see the difference between "I" and "you" messages? Try this trick; you will be amazed at the cooperation you will get.

EXERCISE: *Complete this scenario using "I" statements. A student is disrupting your class while you are trying to teach. You send a couple of nonverbal signals to stop the behavior, but the student ignores you. You ask the student to join you in the hall and say ...*

_____

_____

_____

_____

_____

_____

_____

_____

You might say, "I feel frustrated when you tease other students because it disrupts the class, and neither I nor your friends can concentrate on the lesson. Even if you are not interested in this topic, I want you to stop being so disruptive and respect your peers enough to allow them to learn. Do you think you could please do that for me? I know if you would participate, your contribution would be valuable. Won't you join us? Thanks."

Another simple communication technique is called "reflective listening." This technique involves listening carefully and then paraphrasing what was said and adding what you think the speaker is feeling. For example, if a parent calls and is upset because you did not pass his or her child, listen carefully and then say, "You seem to be very upset because your child failed my class." Suppose the parent corrects you by saying, "No, I'm upset because if you were a better teacher, then my kid would have passed." You respond, "So, you are frustrated because you feel it is my fault that your child failed my class." At this point, the parent might rethink what he or she is saying and try to explain the relevant feelings; if not, this might be a good time to arrange a meeting with the child and parent to review the grades and talk about the problems. This technique works well with all ages and in all situations.

EXERCISE: Your principal comes to you with a complaint. He says, "The amount of noise coming from your room during third period seemed to be excessive. I could hear your students from the other end of the hallway." How might you reply using reflective listening?

Here is a possibility: "I'm sorry that you were upset because my students were noisy. They were so excited and actively engaged in discovery projects. Would you like to join us tomorrow?"

Fishy Fundamentals

Communication is not a one-size-fits-all activity. You should consider tailoring the message to coincide peacefully with the total environment of the receiver. If your receiver is a bottom dweller, then don't float your message on the surface of the water. You must understand the world of your listener before you can effectively communicate.

> *"The true spirit of communication consists in building on another man's observation, not overturning it."*
> *— Edward Bulwer-Lytton*

You might argue, "We all teach at the same school. We share the same environment." That is true, but once again, put on your snorkel gear. Look closely at the differences. Eric Berne[1], the father of the theory of transactional analysis, helped us to understand interpersonal communication. He explained that people communicate with three "ego states." He called these states the parent, the child, and the adult.

Eric Berne developed his theory in 1950, and he compared the mind to a tape recorder that was always recording. Today, we suppose he would have compared the mind to the hard drive of a computer. According to Berne, the parent ego state consists of the "parent tapes" stored in your mind. During your early years, you recorded everything that was said or done by anyone who served in a parental role. If you spent long hours alone in front of the television during this time of development, then you also recorded many media messages. If you were lucky, your parents gave you good, nurturing information, and your tapes say that you are loved and valued. Moral and ethical information along with common sense, safety, and survival material are on your parent tapes. If you were unlucky in the parent department, you might feel devalued or angry.

Child tapes recorded the thoughts, behaviors, and feelings you had as a child. As you can imagine, your child tapes were directly affected by the parenting you received. Hopefully, the good stuff from childhood— like your childlike sense of wonder, optimism, and trust—replays on those tapes. If your childhood was less than perfect, the childhood tapes might play back temper tantrums, jealousy, and distrust.

Your adult ego state is what you have figured out for yourself to be true. It is how you live your life and make your choices. If you are smart, you constantly update your parent and childhood tapes and erase anything that is untrue and not useful. An old story tells about an angler's wife who would always cut a sizable amount off the tail end of a sea bass before she put it in the pan to bake. When her husband questioned her about this wasteful practice, she said that this was the way her mother taught her to bake the bass. When her husband got the chance, he asked his mother-in-law why she cut the end off the fish. She explained that the fish was always too big for her pan, and so she had to slice some off to make it fit. As you can see, the angler's wife didn't examine her child tapes with her adult, logical mind and, consequently, continued to employ useless information.

What does all this talk about ego states and tapes have to do with you and communicating within your school community? Every time you talk to someone, you might hook into his/her parent, child, or adult states depending on what you say, how you say it, and how he/she is feeling. Tell a student to "sit down and shut up," and you might hook into his child state and witness the tantrum a six-foot-tall teen can throw. Be careful that he doesn't hook your child state and engage you in the same behavior. Try to explain a new idea to an old-timer whose parent tapes seem to dominate, and you might get a good old-fashioned lecture. Imagine a teacher in the parent state who wants to talk about how awful the green hair looks on that girl approaching you in the hallway. In your adult state, you might respond that you really don't mind colored hair. The conversation will probably stop because you won't join her in her parent state and agree that kids today are disgraceful.

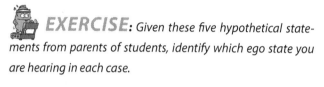 *EXERCISE: Given these five hypothetical statements from parents of students, identify which ego state you are hearing in each case.*

1. *Well, I'm sure my child would not have done anything wrong. I'll just have to report you to the principal!*
   _____

2. *The way most of the girls dress today is disgraceful.*
   _____

3. *I realize my daughter is not performing as well as she might. What do you think I might do to help?*
   _____

4. *My son told me how you embarrassed him in class yesterday. Where do you get off treating him like that?*
   _____

5. *I really appreciate the help you are giving my daughter; thank you so much!* _____

If you decided the above exercises demonstrated (1) parent, (2) parent, (3) adult, (4) child, and (5) adult ego states, then you are right on track.

The only way you can have a productive conversation is if everyone stays in the adult ego state. If someone is communicating from the child state, which hooks your parent state, then you will have a cross transaction, and the communication will break down. Child/child, parent/parent, and adult/adult transactions are the most productive. Ideally, when you are having a conference in an educational setting, you and the parent should both be operating in the adult state. If that is not the case, try to set up a second meeting including another adult, such as your principal or the school counselor. Many times, an objective third party can facilitate a more productive discussion.

Parents, students, teachers, and administrators are swimming in your waters on the same day. Remember they come fully loaded with three ego states and sometimes with heavy emotional baggage. Swim carefully, and always stay alert for that unexpected harpoon.

Becoming a Multilingual Mimic Fish

Since you are now aware of the importance of communication, are you wondering how you fit into the network of fish? Let's first look at the four types of communicators you will encounter among your peers, administrators, and students. No type is better or worse than any other; each is different, and each is needed to provide a well-balanced school environment.

Close to the surface, you will find the fish that like the warmest water: the angelfish and the clown loaches. Angelfish are definitely lovers, not fighters. They are good listeners and do not want to be the boss but are great in a supporting role. They are good at persuasion and seek to be part of a group. These angels have great counseling skills and are caring and thoughtful. They are usually peaceful and calm and are most comfortable in slowly flowing waters. Similarly, clown loaches are dreamers, spontaneous, and always involved; however, they prefer swifter, warm waters and can become very excited. They often dart from one activity to another. They tend to use exaggeration and generalization when communicating and frequently seek praise, whether consciously or not. They, like angelfish, are persuasive and have been known to encourage others into a group hug. These boisterous fish can scare docile fish.

Elsewhere in the pond, where the water is cooler, you find the meticulo fish and the commander fish, independent creatures who appreciate organization and structure. The meticulo fish is somewhat cautious and likes to work alone. A methodical and precise problem solver, this fish greatly enjoys collecting and analyzing data. Although pretending to stay uninvolved in school issues, this fish is superior at asking questions, which allow others to see the problem from a completely different perspective. These fish need a clean, clear environment of slowly moving water. Due to their shy temperaments, they do not like to be isolated with active, fierce fish.

Commander fish like to manage others and tend to be controlling. Active and decisive, these fish remain cool and competitive in times of stress. They do not like to deal with feelings and attitudes and do not care to be given advice. They are quick and impressive when work needs to be done and display good administrative skills. These fish are so active that they have been known to jump out of the water if they feel the environment is too small. They are not fussy about water composition, and they tend to keep to themselves.

EXERCISE: *Do you recognize yourself as one of these four types of fish? Which one do you see yourself as and why?*

_____

_____

_____

_____

_____

_____

_____

_____

_____

Actually, people exhibit attributes of each of these four fish to some extent, so trying to label others and ourselves is simplistic. However, being able to recognize the main types of communicators and to deal with each one appropriately is invaluable as you work with people. If you cannot adapt to the different communicator styles, teaching will be tough for you. You must share your ideas with students, administrators, peers, and parents in a diplomatic manner. Therefore, you must be extremely flexible in how you communicate with others.

Imagine you are attending a party where four different languages are spoken among the guests. Because you speak English, you find it difficult, if not impossible, to interact with those who speak only German, Spanish, or French. You might find yourself drawn to the other English speakers in the group, and you might even feel so uneasy that you leave the party early. However, if you were multilingual, you could interact successfully with everyone at the party. Thus, we might all profit from becoming multilingual mimic fish.

This fish might be any of the four communicator types explained above, but it is capable of masquerading as the others if necessary. In the following paragraphs, you will find pointers on how to become an effective, multilingual mimic fish.

If you are an angelfish, you might be more effective if you try to complete tasks on time, become willing to let others do some work for you, and work hard to say no to many of the frequent demands on your time. This will allow you to concentrate on the important issues. When interacting with angelfish, remember that they get along best with those who actively listen to their points of view and accept their feelings. If you are warm and sincere and seem to appreciate them as team players, they will be much more receptive to your cause.

If you are a clown loach, when working with others you need to control your emotions and your time better. Try to be more objective. Be specific in organizational planning so you can concentrate on the problem at hand and be logical in your approach. If you are working with clown loaches, remember that they appreciate a coworker who does not mind if they occasionally stray from the subject. They respond well to people who are interested  in their dreams and ideas, and they want to avoid quarreling, if possible. They like compliments from others and feel good when you allow them to share their perspectives with you.

If you are a meticulo fish, then you need to be more open and exhibit concern and appreciation for others. Try to relax, and see guidelines as fuzzy boundaries instead of rigid rules. Be accepting of shortcuts to save time or money and of another person's point of view. Be timely in your decision making, and don't get mired down in too many details. When approaching meticulo fish, appreciate how thorough and well prepared they are. Remember, they like to hear tangible and factual evidence. They appreciate time for deliberation and analysis, and they especially like you to notice the accuracy and quality of their work.

If you are a commander fish, you need to practice active listening. Try to appear relaxed, and work on being patient and sensitive. Always show concern for others, and share the reasons for your conclusions. Try to be a team player. To work well with commander fish, you should appreciate how businesslike and efficient they are. Let them know that you value precision, organization, and factual summaries. Do not appear to be primarily driven by emotions.

EXERCISE: *Imagine you are working on a group project with two other people. One of your coworkers is an angelfish and the other a meticulo fish. Together, you must organize Back-to-School Night. It is up to you to set the schedule and notify teachers and parents. Assume you are in charge. How will you approach each one of your coworkers? What particular assignments might go to each one to achieve the best results?*

All three of you should meet and agree on a plan of action. How you deal with your colleagues will depend on your communicator style. Be sure to listen to their ideas and encourage both to be team players. The angelfish might be great at designing the teacher and parent invitations and organizing the hospitality room. His/her warm and caring style will create a welcoming atmosphere. If personal contacts are necessary, this is the worker for you. The  meticulo fish could be very effective in getting the information out to teachers and parents, organizing the timeline, and attending to details to ensure a successful evening (i.e., training student guides, posting signs, outlining traffic flow, etc.).

Be proud of the type of communicator you are while trying to be sensitive to the other types around you. If you get familiar with these communicator types and how to approach each one, you will find school life much more pleasant. If you can relate to a student, parent, or administrator with an appreciation for personal style, you can more effectively communicate with him or her. It's all up to you. Do your homework, and become an effective, multilingual mimic fish.

The Reflection Pool

Reflect on the role of communication in your daily life. What type of communicator is your significant other or your best friend?

Reflect on a disagreement you have had with someone close to you. Can you see where understanding communication may have helped you?

Chapter Three
Fishing for Success

Key Topics:
- **Create a Healthy Habitat**
- **Trusting Fish Will Eat Out of Your Hand**
- **Fast Food Kills Fish**

Create a Healthy Habitat

When you first get an aquarium, you need to prepare the habitat before you introduce the fish, or they will not thrive. You need to be sure the pH of the water is right, the filter is working, and the stones and plants are in place. In much the same way, a functionally designed classroom interior will nurture a positive learning atmosphere.

Chances are your first classroom will be far from ideal. In some situations, you can count your blessings if you have a classroom and don't have to travel from one room to another throughout the day. If you are disappointed with your room, make the most of it without complaining. Use some ingenuity to overcome the obstacles. Good teaching and active learning can occur in the most challenging classroom settings.

Teacher Snapshot

Cindy Harris left her beloved seventh graders and her comfortable classroom to teach science at the high school and to become the head coach for the girls' basketball team. Adjust-

ing to the freshman science curriculum and a new block schedule was a walk in the park compared to not having an assigned classroom. Carting materials from room to room with no place to call her own was a real test for this accomplished teacher.

In her second year of high school teaching, she was assigned to a room that had previously been used to store books. She was elated until she realized that she had to squeeze her desk along with thirty-two student desks and a file cabinet into a twelve-by-thirty-foot windowless room. To make matters worse, there was no chalkboard, bulletin board, or overhead projection screen. The room was empty, except for the loud air-conditioning unit projecting out of a wall, taking up more space.

Cindy had to be innovative to create a positive learning environment. She painted the walls white to cover the stains and to create a screen for her projector. She took the students out of the room whenever she got the opportunity. She used the library for research and the computer lab for virtual science labs. Because she didn't have a demo table, gas, or water to perform wet labs in her classroom, she would borrow other teachers' classrooms. She took the students outside when the curriculum and the weather permitted. Often, Cindy would extend her room into the hallway to create space for group work.

Despite the challenges, Cindy was happy to have a place of her own where she could hang posters, have her own desk, and keep all of her belongings. Her science students thrived in that strange, yet glorious room for two years before she was able to move to a real science classroom.

Cindy's optimistic attitude and good nature served her well in those two years. Her students prospered. Her ability to adjust to adverse circumstances without complaint impressed the faculty and the administration.

To start your interior classroom design, take a moment to think about what you want your classroom to look like. Do you want student desks or tables and chairs? Do you have a choice? Do you want the students to be seated in rows, small groups, or a large circle? Where is your desk? Where will you keep books and supplies? Will you want a reading nook or a conference area? Where is your file cabinet? Do the students need files to keep their work organized?

Now, draw a diagram of your ideal classroom, organized for optimal learning conditions.

With planning and experience, you will improve your classroom design over time (See T.Box: Classroom Design Ideas). The most important thing is that you and your students are comfortable and happy.

TIP: *At the end of the year, keep your eyes and ears open for classroom furniture and supplies you might scavenge for next year. If a teacher is retiring and you like the tables in his room instead of the desks in yours, ask the principal if it's okay to switch. Many times, extra file cabinets are out in the hallway for grabs, or janitors know who has one to give up. After a few years, you'll find you have all the good stuff you need in your room.*

Trusting Fish Will Eat Out of Your Hand

The impression we make in the first thirty seconds of meeting and greeting the students is lasting. Begin with your students in a favorable way. If you leave them with positive feelings, then they will want to come back to your classroom. If you leave them with negative feelings, then you could possibly struggle with annoying behaviors all year.

When students enter your warm and inviting classroom, they don't expect to be greeted by a man-eating shark.

Student Snapshot

Joe, a sophomore new to the school, could not find the classroom he was supposed to be in next. He nervously scuttled along the hallway until he finally saw the correct number above the door. Thank goodness! He quietly entered and slipped into an empty seat near the door. The teacher at the front of the room turned from the blackboard and ceased talking. She pinned her eyes on him.

"Are you a freshman?" she queried.

"No, I'm a sophomore," he answered.

"If you're not a freshman, there is no excuse for being late." she admonished.

An annoying twitter began among the other students, so the teacher raised her voice. "I can hear everything you are saying about me, and I'm used to being called the b-word!"

So began the first day of English class.

Your attitude and approach are extremely important. The learning environment in a classroom must be positive. Students will want to work for you if they respect and trust you. They will grow and thrive in a caring and nurturing environment. Work hard to create and maintain this environment in your classroom, and you will be remembered even after you have left the school. This is a measure of your success.

Golden Moment

A student writes to his industrial arts teacher:

You were one of my favorite teachers because of the way you teach your class and the way you interact with your students to make the class educational and fun at the same time. There are very few teachers that can do that. I learned more in the two years I was in your class than I probably would from anyone else. I just want to thank you for being a great teacher. I now use many of the concepts you taught me in day-to-day life.

Providing a warm, nurturing, and comfortable climate in the classroom will promote smooth water and lead to successful learning. You can establish this climate by cultivating good teacher-student relationships. Begin these relationships by learning your students' names. Talk with your students, and find out about them. Learn about their interests and lives outside the classroom. Be sure to share some things about yourself that will allow your students to see you in a more personal way, not just as an authority figure. Each day, say something positive to each student. You will be surprised how this small investment of time will be invaluable in establishing a trusting relationship. (See T.Box: Ice-Breaker Activities.)

After you know some personal information about the students, and they accept you as a caring mentor, you can work to hook them into learning. Use this personal information to make class work interesting and engaging. For example, if you are teaching a history lesson and know a student is interested in sports, then you might have that student research and report on the sports that were played during that time period. If another student is involved in music, you might ask him/her to play a piece and describe what instruments were popular at the time. These lessons can enrich learning, engage students, and make them feel special. After you have hooked them, you can lead them into developing new areas of interest. Remember, it is important to reach all students, even those who are challenging and appear apathetic.

Golden Moment

In the words of a caring middle-school art teacher:

One of the ninth-grade classes that I taught was careers in art. Most of the students in this class had no desire to be in school. College-bound students were not encouraged to sign up for this class. A class that began with twelve students was down to four by spring break: three had dropped out of school, three transferred to other districts by request, and two moved on to juvenile detention.

We had only a few weeks to finish a project that had been planned with the larger group. The students would paint wall graphics that they as a class had designed around the top of the walls in the commons room, a room that was also used as a lunchroom. All students, present and future, would see this work. It was important to us. Preliminary work was finished and only the fun part was left. My crew enjoyed painting during class, but not one of the four volunteered to stay after school to see that the room got finished by the end of the year. I explain this so you will understand why I picked up a brush to help.

Because the task was easy at this stage, it allowed the students to visit. They talked about everything going on in their lives: dates, breakups, parties, drivers' licenses, and accidents of all kinds. Jim mentioned that he was seventeen and wanted to be an architect.

Without thinking, I reacted. "Seventeen?" The students had forgotten that I was there. Jim admitted without hesitation that he had dropped out of school for two years.

"Well," I said, "it took a lot of guts to come back. Good for you!"

"Oh," he responded, "I had to, or my mom wouldn't let me move home."

I wondered if I could be that strong in the same situation.

"She must love you a lot," I murmured. There was silence for a little while, and then they resumed their talking.

The system would be lucky to keep Jim in school three more years to graduate. What chance did he have, I wondered, of making it through five additional years required for a degree in architecture at the state university?

One nice thing about small schools with small classes is that field trips are easy to coordinate. My four students agreed that, yes, they would like to visit anywhere. Our destination was a technical vocational college about an hour away. There were schools closer, but I knew the teacher of the AutoCAD course and had a special request.

We toured the entire school, but we spent most of our time in the computer lab. The instructor welcomed us and then stepped back to let his students take over with presentations explaining what they were learning, demonstrating the computer programs, and showing us the real projects they were working on for money. A few of those projects were for local architects. When we left the school, my students were excited … about where we would stop for lunch. So much for planting seeds to grow future citizens.

The walls got painted, and school let out for the summer. I would have no more opportunities to reach any of these ninth graders, as they would move into a different building for high school.

The fall school semester began with a surprise visit from Jim. He had come by to tell me that he and his mother had moved and that he was in a different school system. My heart sank.

"My mom moved us so I could go to a high school that offers AutoCAD."

Yes!

Fast Food Kills Fish

Your habitat is comfortable, and your fish trust and respect you and are ready to eat out of your hand. Now is the time to provide nourishment. You don't throw fast food into the tank just because you don't have the time or energy to offer nutritional meals. Of course not, because your fish would soon get sick and probably die. Instead, you research the nutritional needs of your charges and then give the proper food to encourage growth and maintain health.

> *"The fate or fortune of tomorrow's world rests upon our children and how they are taught." — B. C. Forbes*

In your classroom, you should serve only nutritious, meaningful material to your students. You package that between a routine opening and a routine closing, and you have your recipe for success.

Your students will settle in and settle down with a beginning activity each day and will be drawn into your lesson. There are ways to begin your class that will enhance your curriculum. For example, post an essential question on the board each day and have the students begin by writing everything they know about that question. Direct students to write in their journals or to correct a sentence on the board that relates to the lesson for the day. Provide creative puzzles or problem-solving activities to jump-start their brains. These are just a few suggestions for establishing a positive learning environment at the beginning of class. You can probably think of others. (See T.Box: Class Beginning Activities).

EXERCISE: *Record some of your opening activity ideas.*

_____

_____

_____

_____

_____

_____

_____

_____

_____

_____

Once you have started class effectively, you can introduce those meaningful activities (see chapter five) you have planned. Assignments and activities that are varied, engaging, and timed to maximize learning in the classroom will assist you in having a smoothly flowing classroom. Always plan more than you can accomplish in one class period. Have an enrichment activity ready to employ if the students finish early. Remember, busy fish are happy fish, and an idle fin can create waves of mischief.

End the class with a routine that works for you as well as the students. Let the students know that you will indicate when it is time to stop working. Some teachers end the period with a quick quiz over the material just covered. Others like to generate a class discussion to wind up the hour. Perhaps allowing five minutes of unstructured, quiet discussion time might be in order. (See T.Box: Classroom Ending Ideas.)

EXERCISE: *Write down some ways you would like to end class.*

_____

_____

_____

_____

_____

_____

In a nutshell (or should we say seashell), a successful teacher prepares a starting activity each day that will engage students. Be sure your curriculum activities are meaningful and varied. Try to have more than enough planned for each day. Finish the class period in a routine manner that students accept and embrace. Be ready for the unexpected, and keep your sense of humor. Enjoy each day.

 *Student Snapshot*

A teacher had just completed a lesson with his first graders on why not to smoke or do drugs. During the discussion, one little girl tentatively raised her hand. "I just decided to never smoke in my whole life."

The teacher praised her. "That's wonderful. That's a very wise thing to decide."

The other students regarded her with warmth. Bolstered by the positive strokes, the little girl's hand again went up. "Also, I plan never to be a hooker!"

The Reflection Pool

Reflect on classrooms you have experienced that had negative learning atmospheres. Can you now see what was wrong? What will you do in your own classroom to avoid these pitfalls?

Chapter Four

Hooking Students into Learning

Key Topics:
- **Bait-Taking Styles**
- **The Big Three**
- **The Treble Hook**

Bait-Taking Styles

Trout give anglers a thrill with a tug and a run at the fly, unlike catfish, which will nibble and play with the worm before taking the bobber down. Crappie, if in the mood, will take even a bare hook and then lay over on their sides to be obligingly caught. Just like successful anglers know that different kinds of fish take bait in a variety of ways, successful teachers know that students learn in a variety of ways. If you want to enjoy the thrill of the catch and get your students hooked, you must understand learning style preferences.

Let's take a peek into historical research on this subject. The idea of differing learning styles originated in the 1970's and immediately became very popular. There is a strong intuitive appeal to the idea that learner preferences can be important to learning outcomes. In fact, those who teach and those who learn generally accept that planning instruction to adapt to individual preferences does affect how rapidly and how well learners take in new information and ideas.[2]

Being aware of a student's preferred style of learning, gives educators information which facilitates student-teacher interaction and leads to the development of helpful teaching strategies. Learning styles will undoubtedly differ within any one classroom and teachers should adjust how they teach to embrace a variety of styles; even going so far as to include room redesign, small group techniques, and hands on activities.[3]

Being aware of individual learning preferences encourages student involvement in the learning process. It helps them expand and deepen personal learning strategies, strengthens self-awareness and augments knowledge of the thought process and the factors that influence thinking. As your students are challenged to learn in a variety of ways, they become more effective learners.[4]

However, we should not allow information gleaned from measuring learning style preference to limit students, since everyone can learn from most any style, regardless of their personal inclination. It may be more important to match presentation style to the subject itself than to learner preference. And, we as educators must never underestimate the learning variable that outshines all others, the will to learn.[5,6]

In 2009 the Pashler panel surveyed available research and concluded most studies flatly contradict the "meshing hypothesis", which simply stated is *the most effective instruction is that which matches the learning style favored by the learner.* Most of the negative press cited today concerning learning style inventories (LSI's) stems from this particular research. However, this group also pointed out that there was a lack of sound scientific methodology in the study of learning styles and that more and better research was needed. Additionally, it is important to remember, the very process of gaining information about student learning preferences encourages the teacher to be more aware of the styles of teaching they are using. The resulting variety of instruction could be beneficial to all students, regardless of matching. Even if teaching to a learner's best modality cannot be shown to appreciably affect achievement, the most important thing is for the presentation to match the content's best modality. Learning is facilitated when content drives the choice of teaching style.[5,7]

In conclusion, finding little evidence that the "meshing theory" actually works is no surprise. Children are extremely complex and in using them as test subjects, it is impossible to assure the appropriate controls necessary for effective scientific research. Similarly, the lack of support for this theory is no real loss to educators. Anyone who has spent time in a diverse classroom rapidly becomes aware that actually trying to teach a particular lesson to each student in his/her preferred learning modality results in a teaching nightmare! However, using LSI's in the classroom is still a very positive strategy. It allows students to find out more about themselves and the learning process, while it reminds teachers to be sure to use a variety of teaching styles properly aligned with content.

Lucky for you, several different learning-styles inventories are available to help you. Learning-style theory takes into consideration how people perceive and process information in different ways. You cannot analyze each of your students to any great depth; however, you can and should give a simple paper-and-pencil test that distinguishes between the three major perceptual learning styles: visual, auditory, and kinesthetic. (See T.Box: Learning-Styles Inventories.)

The Big Three

The visual learners, the popeyed perch in the school, learn well by seeing information. They need to see the entire picture before they begin learning the details. They are usually good readers and spellers, so giving written directions and assignments from the textbook will work well for them. They

like to take notes in class. Using flowcharts during note taking (See T.Box: Flowcharts for Note Taking) and then teaching students to underline or highlight the major ideas in different colors helps them to remember. They respond well to visual aids such as the smartboard, graphics, films, diagrams, cartoons, and flash cards. Encouraging students to visualize or picture words and concepts is helpful. Visual learners pick up meaning from the teacher's facial expressions and body language. These learners usually like a quiet learning environment.

The sonar salmon, the auditory learners, learn best by hearing rather than reading information. If they say a fact aloud, they learn it better. Jingles and mnemonic devices are helpful to their learning because most enjoy listening to music. Encourage the use of singsong memory devices (See T.Box: Memory Devices). Lectures, recordings, and reading aloud help these learners to focus. Taking lecture notes and frequently reviewing the material is extremely helpful.

Auditory learners like giving oral presentations and participating in class discussions. Small-group discussions and one-on-one interviews that relate directly to class material also benefit these learners. For example, when studying the Vietnam War, an auditory learner might benefit from interviewing a Vietnam War veteran and then giving an oral report to the class.

The kinesthetic learner, the frisky filefish, learns through touching, moving, and doing. Muscle movement is necessary for creating long-term memories. A short attention span is common in kinesthetic learners, so they are most successful with hands-on activities. They enjoy working with objects and get easily distracted if they are not allowed to explore and experiment. These students will learn best with projects, field trips, labs, demonstrations, and role-play. Gum chewing and listening to music could actually help these kinesthetic learners concentrate.

 Student Snapshot

Tony was definitely a kinesthetic learner. He worked best when seated at the front of the room, where there were fewer distractions. He wiggled in his seat and had a habit of tapping his pencil when he was thinking through the coursework. Although the other students became accustomed to his ways, it was always difficult when a guest speaker came into the classroom. We discovered that giving this young man a stress ball to knead during a presentation limited his distracting activities and made the atmosphere more comfortable for the speaker.

Useful kinesthetic teaching strategies might include making models, conducting labs, and role-playing. Hands-on activities are great. Have students trace letters, words, and pathways. Encourage them to use the computer. They should work with term cards and walk when memorizing. Allow them to express ideas through dance or drama. They can repeatedly write facts to be learned and make study sheets. Help them look for associations between class material and real life. Have them use all five senses in fun, trial-and-error activities (See T.Box: Trial-and-Error Activities).

Be sure to choose one of the learning-style inventories from the free downloadable resources in T.Box available on our website to try with your students. You will find that most students utilize all three learning styles to some degree, but one may be dominant. Take time to analyze the results with your class. It will help everyone to better understand his/her unique learning preferences, and you will have the right bait to hook learners.

The Treble Hook

Many times, we teachers teach the way we learn best because it worked for us. Although somewhat logical, this is not the best approach. The only way we can efficiently get the subject matter across to our students is to consider all three learning styles within our presentation format. A good teacher must find out how students learn, choose the teaching style which matches the concept being taught, and include activities that embrace each modality in the daily lesson plans.

Like the angler who employs a treble hook, a device with three separate hooks fashioned into one, you should always include a hook for the popeyed perch, the sonar salmon, and the frisky filefish, respectively, in your tackle box of teaching tactics. Remember, it does not hurt a visual learner to do an auditory or kinesthetic activity, or vice versa. All students can do the same activities; just make sure you have some activities to suit each type of learner for each lesson you teach, and insure they are enhancing to the material. (See T.Box: Lesson Plan Template.) It might be helpful to go through a lesson so you can see how this works. Assume you are teaching to the following objective: *students will be able to identify the major parts of the human heart and explain its function, including the blood-flow pathway.* The following sample lesson plan includes a variety of activities for all three types of learners and accomplishes your objective.

Parts and Function of a Human Heart

Introduction: Present a short (no more than twenty minutes) lecture on the topic by utilizing PowerPoint or a document reader. Point out the major parts of the heart on the visual aids, explain their functions, and trace the path of blood flow through the heart. You might want to show a YouTube video of a real heart in action. Following this presentation, encourage students to ask questions and discuss the information. This appeals to visual learners because they see the appropriate terms on the whiteboard along with the heart itself and the blood-flow pathway. It appeals to auditory learners because they hear each term pronounced properly, and they hear the blood-flow pathway explained. They listen to student questions and can clarify information for themselves aloud during the question/answer session. In addition, twenty minutes is not too long for the kinesthetic learners to sit still and pay attention.

Review of Concepts: Allow students (preferably your kinesthetic learners) to come up to the graphic and physically touch it to trace the blood-flow path while verbalizing, in correct order, the parts of the heart the blood passes through. Encourage students (possibly through extra credit) to create a replication of the blood pathway through a drawing or clay model.

Handout and Homework: Give out a list of relevant terms that the students are expected to master, along with a homework assignment from the text, due the next day, that correlates well with the subject matter. This homework will appeal primarily to visual learners, but auditory and kinesthetic learners should be able to do it competently after the classroom work is completed, as they will already be familiar with the material.

Activity: Have each student make his/her own set of term cards from the list of relevant terms (three-by-five-inch note cards work great). Each card should have the term alone on one side and a definition or explanation of the term in words or pictures on the other side. These are individualized card sets. Students should put the definitions in their own words and/or drawings. Allow students to choose how to complete this activity. Visual learners may prefer to work individually with their textbooks. Auditory and kinesthetic learners might prefer to work in a small group, discussing each term and referring to the visual resources under the teacher's guidance. Students who finish their term cards early can work on the homework assignment in class until the others have caught up.

Review: Have the students quietly study their cards for five minutes. They should look at each term, say the definition to themselves first, and then check the back of the card to see if they are correct. This will help visual and kinesthetic learners. Then, allow five minutes of study aloud with a partner. This will facilitate learning for auditory and kinesthetic learners.

Handout: Provide worksheets of the human heart with no labels of major parts and no marked path of blood flow. Have the students attempt to label the parts and draw the flow path from memory. Allow them to finish the worksheet with the aid of their term cards so they are sure to complete it accurately.

Collect Work: Have students turn in all work done during class, except the homework. Look over the term-card sets and worksheets and give completion points in the grade book.

Quiz: End with a quick quiz, maybe matching or fill-in-the-blank questions.

Homework Due: Remind students the homework will be collected at the start of the next class period. This assignment will reinforce classroom learning. Even if some students do not do the homework, they have still learned the concept. The student's grade will be lower, but he or she will not be lost.

"Education is not received. It is achieved." — Anonymous

Giving a learning-styles inventory is a great way to start the year. It allows discussion, and you begin to get to know the students through a fun activity. They feel relaxed in your class and enjoy learning about themselves. Try hard to include activities for all three types of learners. It will be obvious from these activities that you see the students as individuals and that you care about each one of them. Have fun with this, and you will not regret your efforts.

"Man's mind stretched to a new idea never goes back to its original dimensions."
— Oliver Wendell Holmes, Jr.

The Reflection Pool

Choose a concept you will be teaching. Using the treble-hook approach, design activities that you might use in class to keep all students actively learning.

Hooking Students into Learning

Chapter Five

Gone Fishin'— Curriculum and Activities

Key Topics:

- Successful Angler Essentials
- Nutritious Bait and Fishbowl Routine
- Plan to Catch Your Limit

Successful Angler Essentials

It is important to recognize that there is no one right way to fish. Successful anglers know when the fish are biting and use their favorite type of rod and reel. They swear by their special kinds of bait, and they practice casting until they perfect their technique.

"To be a successful fisherman, you should get there when the fish are biting." — Anonymous

Similarly, there is no one right way to teach. Think of all the different teachers you have experienced during your school career. Despite their differences, as long as the teachers could encourage and motivate students, learning occurred.

What is essential for you as the teacher? Each classroom should reflect the teacher's personality and attitude toward education. Do not be afraid to make your classroom your own. You will be able to relax and enjoy this job if you create a learning community in which you, as well as your students, are comfortable.

Teacher Snapshot

At the beginning of her first year of teaching, Becky James, a science teacher, found her classroom next door to Jeff Carter, a well-established language arts teacher. Becky quickly observed that Jeff had complete control over his classroom at all times. Students did not speak out of turn, seemed to be on task, and always had their supplies. It was very quiet and orderly in the classroom, and the lessons flowed smoothly. Jeff was obviously a good teacher. He was respected by other teachers and by students (although some students did not like the classroom structure very much).

Becky decided her classroom should be like Jeff's. Yet, when she tried to effect order, nothing seemed to work right. The students would not be quiet during science activities. Someone always forgot a pencil or could not find homework in his/her book bag. Students felt free to joke and relax. She worried they were not taking their studies seriously enough. Becky fought and struggled for the entire first year, trying hard to emulate Jeff. No matter how hard she tried, she couldn't maintain the strict environment and felt like a stranger in her own classroom. She thought she was a poor teacher, and she wasn't having any fun.

Finally, with a little experience under her belt, she got brave enough to accept that maybe her classroom could be different but just as effective as her neighbor's. She vowed to make the science classroom more in tune with her personality. The next year, she discovered she was really a good teacher! The students enjoyed science and learned well. Did they visit during labs, joke, and tease some? Yes, but that was okay. As long as Becky was comfortable in the environment, the students were learning, and no one was being disrupted, things were fine. She had changed the classroom to fit her personality.

You will develop your personal teaching style over time as you gain classroom experience. For now, simply opening yourself up to the idea that there is no one right way to teach is invaluable and liberating.

> *"Education is not filling a bucket, but lighting a fire!"* — *William Butler Yeats*

What is essential for your students? A good teacher is encouraging. When students feel good about themselves, they will try harder and achieve more. Look for the positive and identify individual talents.

 **Golden Moment**

Upon retirement, a dedicated teacher (of language arts), who was already a certified counselor, began a counseling practice. One day, a woman brought her daughter in for counseling. The woman introduced herself and explained, "You may not remember me, but I was in your language arts class my freshman year of high school. You read one of my essays aloud to the class as an example of good work. That meant so much to me. I'm just sure you can help my daughter."

Recognize effort. Giving completion points along with a score for accuracy can leave those weaker students with a sense of dignity and the encouragement to try again. Say something constructive before mentioning where improvement might be made. It works well to focus on the deed, not the doer; analyze the work done, not the person that did it. The lasting effects on student effort in the classroom are created more by how you say something than by what you say. You could say, "This paragraph needs a few more supporting details. How could some of those be included?" Or you could say, "You have left out supporting details here. You need to add some." Which is more encouraging?

Don't scold or reprimand students continually; this is not encouraging. The more times students hear a complaint, the less they will pay attention to it. It is fine to repeat your requirements for an assignment to the group several times, but do not single out and repeatedly correct someone. The student will be chastising himself or herself enough without you adding to it, or he or she will have learned early on how to tune you out.

Give the students your undivided attention. This in itself is very encouraging.

 Student Snapshot

A small girl approached the teacher's desk early in the day while the teacher was preoccupied with grading. She asked the teacher, "How do you spell 'hate'?" The teacher absently replied with the spelling, wondering briefly what the student was up to but too busy to pursue the matter. Later that day, the same kid approached the desk and left a note for the teacher. The note read, "I hate you."

Some teachers will give an assignment to the class and then ask for classroom silence so they can grade yesterday's papers. Given limiting circumstances, students who need help will likely not ask for it and will probably not do well on the assignment. Do your grading on your own time, or try grading papers as a group. Students grading one another's papers often results in class discussion and can provide a powerful learning opportunity. You will get foundational concepts across to some learners and get the grading done at the same time.

Let students know what you appreciate. If neatness and punctuality are high on your list, note that on the work when a student has turned in a neat paper on time. If you value creativity, encourage it when you see it. A student might give an answer to a question that is incorrect within your parameters but is very creative. Praise the student for that. An answer can have degrees of rightness and wrongness. Encouraging kids to think outside the box is important.

If students want to tackle a task that you think may be beyond their capability, you might let them try. Be sure they know you are available to help when they need it. Students will retain and remember more if they find their own way to learning and are not spoon-fed. They will either realize they are in over their heads and be ready for further information, or they may surprise you and complete the task well.

Your respect is very encouraging. Be respectful of students. If their work is not up to your standard, have an example ready to show the students what you expect. Try to praise what has been done, and then ask them what more could be done to improve the work. If you maintain a kind and caring approach, focus on the work, and offer constructive criticism in encouraging language, the result will be the beginning of a positive learning cycle.

> "The mediocre teacher tells. The good teacher explains.
> The superior teacher demonstrates. The great teacher inspires."
> — William A. Ward

Good teachers are motivational. They stimulate students to learn and to fulfill their individual potentials. A motivational teacher sees untapped resources and taps into them. Instead of getting angry when a student is doodling on his paper, check out those doodles. Are they good? Many times shy, artistic students will give themselves away with their scribbles. These students can become more motivated in your class if you use their talent to your advantage. Ask such a student to do some illustrations for the bulletin board. Let it become obvious that you are proud of that talent.

 **Student Snapshot**

In the words of an expert biology teacher:

Charles was a very talented, young football player. Let's just say if it weren't for football, this young man probably would not have stayed in school. During the football season, with a little help from his coach, he seemed to stay motivated, complete his homework, and earn a passing grade. Shortly after football season ended, his grades dropped drastically. I talked to him several times, trying to figure out what actually motivated him to do well.

One day, as the students were getting ready for class, I noticed Charles unpacking photos and carefully placing them on his table. I was afraid to look, thinking they might be photos of naked young ladies. To my surprise, they were photos of Charles in his football uniform.

I asked him why he brought photos of himself in uniform. He replied, "I did so well during football season wearing my football jersey; I just thought this would motivate me to do well."

I laughed and said, "Can we get a poster size to hang in every room?" This certainly was a priceless moment in education and a clear indication of doing "whatever it takes to motivate."

A key to engaging or motivating students is to recognize that everyone wants to feel successful. Some students, however, have experienced failures in learning, and they may no longer be motivated to attempt learning activities. A few students will not risk contributing information or answering questions for fear of looking silly in front of their peers. Others are so meticulous that they will never produce anything of quality by their standards; thus, they continue to refine and, consequently, do not turn in assignments. Some students cannot engage or focus on their work because of turmoil in their lives.

As an effective teacher, you must assume there are reasons for lack of motivation or engagement. Discover the reasons, and then use that information to help each child become successful. The following story of a teacher who misread Sarah's lack of effort as being lazy or apathetic is important to share.

 ***Student Snapshot***

Sarah was sent to the office for falling asleep in class. The teacher wrote on the incident card that Sarah did not pay attention in class and was not doing her homework. While talking with Sarah about why she was inattentive and not doing her homework, the principal heard a sad and alarming story. Each night, Sarah shoved a dresser against her bedroom door and kept a knife under her pillow. She stayed awake to keep her mother's boyfriend from molesting her and her little sister. Additional help was provided to Sarah and her sister after the case was reported to the state hotline for abuse.

In this case, the teacher ultimately helped Sarah by sending her to the office. What would have happened if Sarah had not trusted her principal enough to tell the truth? How much more quickly could this problem have been resolved if Sarah's teacher had established a trusting relationship and assumed there was a reason for her lack of effort? Try hard to build relationships as early as possible, and don't be afraid to invite a student to confide in you.

> *"A good teacher is one whose ears get
> as much exercise as his mouth." — Anonymous*

High expectations coupled with achievable standards foster motivation. You can help students master concepts in several different ways. One technique is to break the idea down into smaller learning units. Another way is to take time after school to help a student to grasp a key concept.

If you find it difficult to provide individual encouragement and motivation within a conventional classroom, try setting up your room to foster the concept of community. Separate your class into small work groups. This will facilitate discussion and reinforce learning. Student discussion can sometimes put a spin on the information that you had not thought about. Within the group, students help one another to understand the concepts. The learning community also increases  student commitment. Students take ownership for success within their groups because they feel like they belong and are accepted. While this learning community can be very beneficial, some students might be too immature or inexperienced to handle the environment initially. You must be sure to provide an adequate foundation and guidelines when setting up the learning community to assure it can become a success. (See T.Box: Learning Communities.)

Always be flexible and open to creative ways of approaching the subject. Try to keep learning fun and exciting for yourself and your students. You will be surprised at the pride you and your students will take in the achievements you accomplish together.

Nutritious Bait and Fishbowl Routine

Because mandatory assessment is the norm, it is important to teach the required curriculum, or your students will not do well when tested even if they have learned a great deal. Your choices about what you teach are limited, but how you teach the material is up to you. The basic information can be taught in many different ways and can be interesting or boring, depending on how you present it and how relevant you make it to the students.

Students are receptive to meaningful, not meaningless, activities. For an activity to be meaningful, to be nutritious, it must be understandable, challenging, and directly related to the learning objective. Students sometimes see activities as meaningless if they are redundant or appear to be busy work. Some activities can appear overwhelming to students because they are too long or difficult for the students to accomplish in a timely manner; consider breaking these into smaller parts.

 Teacher Snapshot

Mr. Jones was an American history teacher who had taught for more than twenty years. Every year, he used the same assignment, which consisted of three yellow sheets of paper with specific questions and fill-in-the-blank statements relating to a particular chapter in the textbook. This assignment was worth a lot of points. Students were given four class periods to find all the answers. They were to work quietly and alone. (Notice, this allowed Mr. Jones to sit at his desk for four periods and grade papers. He was fastidious and did not like to have

ungraded papers lying around his desk.) For some visual learners, this might have been a meaningful activity. Auditory and kinesthetic learners, however, found it much too difficult and boring. Because Mr. Jones gave this same assignment every year, the answers were available to those who cared enough to get them. Also, students copied from others just to get it done and then wasted their time in class. This had become a meaningless and outdated activity.

Think about the meaningful activities and assignments you can employ to maximize learning. You need to have multiple and creative ways to facilitate learning. A twenty-minute lecture with graphics might be a great way to get the basic concept across to many students at one time, but if it goes on for half an hour or more, most students will quit paying attention. Colleges of education are trying to get away from the lecture format for presenting information. Edgar Dale[8] introduced his "cone of learning" and research confirms that students retain only 10 percent of what they read, 20 percent of what they hear, 30 percent of what they see, 50 percent of what they see and hear, 70 percent of what they discuss, and almost 90 percent of what they do. Take some time to think about all the ways you could relay foundational knowledge, as well as help the students make connections to their prior knowledge and experiences. These connections are important for retaining and using the knowledge learned in class.

Classroom routine is greatly stressed to elementary teachers, but it is equally important for middle school and high school teachers. You have already been introduced to using routine to frame your daily classroom lessons with positive starting and ending activities. Routines can also be utilized within the middle of each class to produce a classroom atmosphere of familiarity and safety. When students know what is expected of them, they will feel more secure and less likely to exhibit behaviors that have a negative effect on classroom learning.

There are many ways to incorporate routine into the classroom, including using the same method to turn in and distribute papers. When giving an exam, have the next unit syllabus ready so that after students complete the exam they can begin working quietly on the new unit. Even dealing with difficult behavior can be handled in a routine manner. For example, if a student does not turn in homework, make it a habit to hand that student an "Instead of Homework" card (See T.Box: Instead of Homework Cards). This card forces the student to think about why the work was not done and to choose a follow-up behavior. The student must write an explanation and indicate what he or she will do to make up the work. Be sure the student signs the card. If the explanation is reasonable and the student chooses to turn in the work the next day, then remember to ask for the assignment and say thank you when you get it.

Plan to Catch Your Limit

Careful planning can make the difference between a coherent unit and chaos. So, plan, plan, plan! Write down the plan, and adjust it until you can see a great teaching unit emerge. Most problems in the classroom arise from lack of teacher planning. Do not try to shortchange this part of your job. Will you be working overtime that first year? You bet. However, the next year will be much easier and more fun as you adjust and improve on your basic plans. Do not use the same activity for the rest of your teaching career. You will retain your enthusiasm if you look at what you have done previously and then try something new. Ideally, it would be wonderful to journal each day about what did and did not work. Realistically, at least find a moment to make a few notes on the teacher's copy of the activity with changes for next time. This will allow you to grow and develop as the years fly by.

"Insanity: the belief that one can get different results by doing the same thing." — *Albert Einstein*

Variety is the spice of life and of teaching. Try to vary your approach to the topic so students don't get bored and restless. Make a real effort to use your textbook wisely. Use those great techniques you have learned in college. Make up those anticipation guides and three-level study guides. Teach your students two-column note taking to facilitate real learning. Be sure to preview the material and utilize activities to keep your classes interesting and fun. Paired reading activities and "What Do I Know?" sheets keep up student interest and augment understanding. Class discussion should be maximized. MAX Teaching has many anticipation guides free on its Web site, along with a wealth of ideas for motivating students and enhancing learning. (See T.Box: MAX Teaching.)

It is good to alternate bookwork with verbal discussions, labs, artwork, and other fun activities. Do not be afraid to be creative and try something new. If an idea fails, you can always throw it out or revise it. Be sure to have activities that appeal to boys as well as girls. Include activities that highlight or integrate different cultures into the classroom.

Try to have something that appeals to each major type of learner in each lesson plan. You might even ask the students for suggestions of creative ways to assimilate the academic material. They will have some great ideas; after all, they are the ones responsible for learning the material.

EXERCISE: Start a list, here and now, of some potential activities that correlate well with your academic material. Add to this list as you pick up new ideas throughout the school year.

_____

_____

_____

_____

_____

_____

_____

_____

_____

"Ideas are like rabbits. You get a couple and learn how to handle them, and pretty soon you have a dozen." — John Steinbeck

The Reflection Pool

This chapter focused on establishing your comfort level, providing encouragement and motivation to your students, using routines, and maintaining high expectations and achievable standards. Choose three of these ideas, and explain how you will implement them in your classroom..

Chapter Six
Celebrate Fish Diversity

Key Topics:
- **Variety Abounds**
- **A Closer Look**
- **Watch Out for Predators**

Variety Abounds

If you look closely at all the fish in a fishbowl, you will first notice the different colors, sizes, and shapes. If you take time to study the fish, you will begin to notice the different behaviors of each species and the interaction among the fish. Some fish swim for cover the minute you come near. Some hide in the rocks or in the little sea castle that decorates the tank. Other fish don't mind jumping out of the water in hopes that you are bringing food. Some fish pay no attention to you. Sometimes, you will notice that a fish is missing a fin or has a deformed tail. You might notice that certain fish are shunned or bullied by the others.

Much like life in the fishbowl, you will have students of different colors, sizes, shapes, and personalities in your classroom, despite the fact that they are approximately the same age and are from the same species. You will have students who are quiet and shy and try to be invisible. You will have the loud, boisterous ones who always want your attention. You will have some with noticeable physical problems and some, you will begin to realize, with mental and emotional limitations.

For the most part, you can all live relatively peacefully in your fishbowl, but you will have to make accommodations for those few students in each group who need some special treatment. Be alert for students who have difficulty staying on task, obeying the rules, or socializing. Don't write these students off as bad kids by sending them to the office or ignoring them. Think about the possible reasons for the behaviors so you can address the students' needs. Everyone wants to learn and feel like they belong.

"Children are like wet cement; whatever falls on them makes an impression." — Dr. Haim Ginott

Within the first week or two, you will be able to identify your special students. These students may exhibit one or more obvious behaviors that identify them as different from the others. They may be easily distracted and disorganized and may never turn in their work. They might be always talking and never sitting still, or they might be very quiet. Some students will be argumentative, especially with authority figures or preoccupied with death, drawing dark images and writing melancholy poetry. You may notice a student who frequently becomes overwhelmed or feels sick and asks to leave the classroom. Whatever the symptoms, it soon becomes obvious that these students are dealing with more serious problems than the average student.

Your must understand that the student's behavior is the byproduct of the distress and not an intentional distraction for you. Your job is not to diagnose but to be understanding and knowledgeable. Talk to the student, the student's parents, the school counselor, and the school nurse. Try to find out what is going on and how you can help.

A Closer Look

This closer look is designed to help you develop teaching strategies that will enable your special students to learn alongside the others and not become a negative influence in your classroom. Each section begins with a snapshot of a particular type of student behavior and is followed by some classroom strategies designed to help you reach these special students.

Average Joe

Joe is just a normal kid with good and bad days like all of us. Most days, Joe enjoys school, follows the rules, participates in class and regularly turns in homework. But on the bad days, when Joe feels ignored, he will become a Darter, a Flounder, a Bullhead or a Tuned-out Fish just to get attention. He knows how to get what he needs.

Classroom Strategies: Average Joes are often taken for granted by the teacher, whose time and energy is mostly devoted to the special needs of a few students. Don't neglect your Average Joes. They too can feel devalued and unappreciated if they are always expected to comply with classroom norms without your positive, individual attention. Make a special point to recognize their accomplishments and sense of responsibility. Don't force them to assume another identity for you to see them.

Smarty Pants Fish

Brad could read at the second grade level when he entered kindergarten. He also knew how to add and subtract and he could point out the location of any state on the map. Socially and emotionally he was still five years old, but academically he was eight.

Classroom Strategies: It is very important for a teacher to meet the needs of their Smarty Pants Fish. You don't want to be the reason Brad loses interest in school because he is bored. You have to approach each lesson with Brad in mind. Class work, projects and homework should expand Brad's knowledge and challenge him. Administer a routine pre-test for each of your units so you can gauge how much Brad already knows and then expand the subject for him with special projects or readings. In math, you could teach your basic concept for the day, for example, one digit multiplication, and then give Brad two, three or four digit problems, depending on his understanding. You could also use www.khansacademy.org for his accelerated math instruction. In science, you could enlist Brad to design a demonstration of the concept to share with the class. In language arts, Brad could write a song, poem, script or video of the story that your class is reading, or he could read a second story with the same theme and compare the two. Capitalize on the interests and strengths of your Smarty Pants students and they will remain enthusiastic and motivated.

Tuned Out Fish

> *Claire's total attention is focused on scraping off the metallic blue polish on her thumb nail. She turned her nose up at your bait within a few minutes of your lesson and the odds of enticing her back near your hook are astronomical. Claire lost interest after the first few weeks of school. She turns in half of her assignments and most are not completed. She fails tests and her participation in classroom discussions and activities are minimal and sometimes destructive. If confronted, she often will do one of three things: ignore you and not respond; say that she doesn't care; or, agree to put in more effort, but doesn't.*

Classroom Strategies: First of all, you have to know the reasons why Claire has disengaged. You have to understand her home and school life and know her individual abilities, attitudes, strengths and weaknesses. Talk to Claire, her family, the school counselor and social worker to find out about her personal stressors. Check her school files for academic information and her performance history. Once you identify the source of Claire's problem, you will be able to address her needs.

If you understand that Claire has stress at home, you can implement strategies to help. For example, if her family is going through a divorce, she is probably spending a few days with her mom and a few days with her dad. It is also probable that Claire's parents are nervous and confrontational with each other, which creates a stressful environment in both homes. Getting homework completed under these circumstances can be problematic. If this is the situation, you might arrange for a special quiet time during the day for Claire to catch up on her work so she won't get behind. If Claire is in the upper grades, you can use the "Instead of Homework Cards" (see T.Box) and make arrangements for her to turn in the assignment later. Be creative, flexible and empathetic in helping your turned-out fish through this stressful time. Remember, basic needs must be met before a person can concentrate on other matters . . . such as learning.

If you discover that the school environment is the problem because Claire is feeling threatened, teased, disrespected or excluded, then you have to step up, stop the negative behavior of her classmates and create safe classroom opportunities so she experiences success when she participates. One idea, called the "eight raised hands" technique by Rick Smith[9], promotes classroom discussion. The teacher requires eight hands to be raised before anyone is called upon. All eight students give their response and the teacher responds with "thank you" after their answers, then the teacher shares the correct answer. Students are guaranteed that there won't be negative feedback if they participate. Another idea is to give non-judgmental responses like: that's an interesting idea;

interesting, but if you were hanging upside down, could you see the problem in a different way?; you are on the right track, but not quite there yet; you are getting close . . . keep thinking. This will help students feel that they are a valuable member of your class and it will promote participation and higher level thinking.

Students who have experienced success academically believe they can master new material and are motivated to work. Students who have struggled and have not experienced success don't believe in their abilities to learn new material and that translates into low motivation. Research shows[10], *self-efficacy*, a student's belief about his/her ability to master meaningful material, is directly related to motivation.

Some beliefs that interfere with self-efficacy[11] include:

- ❖ The work isn't important or doesn't relate to their lives.
- ❖ They will fail.
- ❖ They will not be cool if they show effort and interest.
- ❖ Their learning problems make it too difficult to keep up.
- ❖ The material is too easy... no challenge, boring... why bother?
- ❖ Appearing helpless will garner needed attention.
- ❖ Emotional distress, such as depression or anxiety, makes learning impossible.
- ❖ Passive aggressive behavior to rebel against parents or teachers is more important than achievement.

Maybe you discover that Claire has low self-efficacy. If you can identify the belief that is interfering with her progress, you can work to update and revise her thinking and help her to step out of that mental trap that is keeping her down.

Once you have figured out why your Tuned-out Fish has

disengaged, address the problem. Bring in community support if the student's problems are beyond the classroom. Do what you can to accommodate personal stressors at school. Revise your lessons so that your students feel like they are doing important work that is useful and relevant. Challenge yourself to make sure that each student feels like a valuable member on your team and their participation is important for the success of the learning activity.

Bullhead

On the return bus ride from a field trip, the bus driver noticed that Sam was standing up in the aisle and told him to sit down. In support of the driver, the teacher also told Sam to be seated. When Sam got up again, the bus driver pulled over to the side of the road and told him to move to a front seat. Sam refused, saying that he wasn't out of his seat, despite the fact that several students said they saw him standing. He held the entire bus hostage for several minutes because he wouldn't move to the front. Finally, his peers pressured him to move. He rode for several miles with his hand in the air and his fist clenched in defiance. When questioned later about his behavior, he said that he was right and that the bus driver and the other kids were wrong. He would not take responsibility for his actions, and he appeared to enjoy the negative attention.

Classroom Strategies: The best way to work with the bullheads in your classroom is to not argue with them. Listen to what they say, and consider their side of the argument. Tell them that you understand what they are saying. If possible, give them choices so they feel that they have some control. In the example above, the bus driver eliminated any choice in the matter, which made the student completely (surprise!) bullheaded. If the driver had given

Sam the choice to sit either up front or with the teacher, then the student would have felt like he had some control, which would have eased the situation.

> *"Always listen to the opinions of others. It may not do you much good, but it will possibly be good for them."* — Anonymous

Darter

Todd was always moving and talking. He had trouble finding anything in his horribly disorganized binder. Often, he would not turn in his homework, and when he did, it was common for his papers to look like they had been wadded up in the wastebasket before they were retrieved and turned in. Todd never seemed to be able to pay attention. Any noise or activity caught his attention and took him away from the lesson. The teacher also noticed that it was especially hard for Todd to work independently on a project; he would always find someone to talk to or to distract.

Classroom Strategies: Try to create novel, stimulating lesson plans. The darters in your classroom are bright, but their brains need to be stimulated to stay focused. You need to include activity, personal interaction, and movement. Allow the class to get up and stretch. Find a chore for the darters to do if they are having trouble staying seated. Make sure that your lessons are structured and that important points are highlighted. Because organization and attention are problems for darters, you should provide a lecture outline to help them take notes (See T.Box: Sample Lecture Outlines). Make instructions short, specific, and direct, because it is almost impossible for darters to follow directions that involve several steps. Ask darters to repeat the directions to you, and don't get upset when you have to repeat the instructions a few times. Creating learning circles or assigning peer helpers is beneficial for the darter. It is especially helpful for the darters when you post the daily schedule and homework assignments.

Darters need to be seated where there are minimum diversions because they are easily distracted. Sounds of heaters and air conditioners and sights through windows and doorways will capture their attention and take the focus away from the lesson. It is best to seat them in front of the class so they won't see other students. Study carrels for tests or for silent reading are especially helpful for darters.

Because organization is such a problem for the darters, you should provide a classroom file with folders. Teach the students how to use the files and help them on a regular basis to stay organized. You will probably want to make the files and folders available to the rest of your students who want them so that it doesn't look like you are giving special treatment to a few.

Darters require regular praise and encouragement. Intangible, long-term rewards are not effective motivators. It is important to discipline the darters and all other students in the same manner. Avoid sarcasm; it is almost always counterproductive with all varieties of fish.

Flounder

Jenny was quiet and sometimes invisible in the classroom. She was easily distracted and always had difficulty completing a task that involved several steps. She never asked for help, despite the fact that she didn't often hand in her homework and was close to failing. When asked about her assignment, Jenny would often say that she did the assignment but forgot to hand it in or couldn't find it. One time when the teacher called her bluff and helped her go through her messy, unorganized binder to find her

paper, he was surprised to find that she had completed the assignment. In other classes where the teachers forgot about Jenny, she would get so far behind in her work that she eventually just gave up.

Classroom Strategies: Although the darters are hyper and in your face and the flounders are quiet and sometimes invisible, they are remarkably similar in their classroom performance. You will find that the classroom strategies that work for the darters will also work for the flounders. Be careful to notice your flounders. Don't let darters consume your attention because then the flounders will fail to thrive.

You will notice that some students isolate themselves from you and others, some become very negative, some are moody, and others seem worried or nervous all of the time. We refer to these as solo fish.

Solo Fish

John always dressed in black and slumped when he walked. He sat by himself, and he never smiled or made eye contact with others. He would write about death and draw pictures of skulls and bloody knives.

Sarah was a beautiful sixteen-year-old girl despite her twelve piercings and purple-tipped hair. Sometimes, she would come into class all smiles—friendly, talkative, and engaging—but within the hour, she could become sullen, quiet, and angry. Her friends never knew what to expect from her. Some called her Jekyll and Hyde behind her back.

Jackie, pale and trembling, would

often approach the teacher and ask to see the nurse. She would refuse to read aloud or do any type of public speaking in class. She was absent from school at least one day each week, and she would never ask the teacher for make-up work.

If Carrie wasn't careful, her long sleeve would push up on her arm, and the red jagged razor cuts would expose her secret.

Classroom Strategies: You can tell that something bad is going on with John, Sarah, Jackie, and Carrie, but you don't know for sure what they are dealing with. Probably, you are not trained to help with something this serious. The best bet is to ask the school counselor to visit with these students and contact their parents. In the classroom, you should engage the students in conversation and encourage their participation in activities. Be flexible with your expectations; too many demands on these students can increase feelings of failure. You might need to modify an assignment or give them some extra time until they start feeling better. Don't nag them about their homework. Be compassionate and caring. Focus more on guiding them to a professional and getting them on the road to recovery, and less on their academic performance. Keep things in perspective.

Grass Carp

Jeremy looks at you through bloodshot eyes and has a silly, crooked smile on his face. You ask him to read aloud a passage in the book, but he can't find the place. When he does start reading, he makes some pronunciation mistakes, and others laugh. You notice that the other students are snickering and talking about him.

Classroom Strategies: It is very important that you do not ignore the grass carp that comes high to your class. Many of the other students know that the student is high. If you don't address the problem, then they will think that you are too stupid to notice or that you are okay with it, and they have permission to do the same. Ideally, you have a strategy in place that will address the problem without disrupting the class and without putting you into an adversarial role.

A strategy that has worked well many times for us, requires some preparation for novice teachers. Sometime in the first few weeks of school, visit with the school nurse. Set up a plan to send any of your students to him/her if you suspect one is high. You may even establish a code word that you can put on the request note asking the nurse to send for your student. The nurse can then check the student and determine the next step. After you have arranged with the nurse in advance, you are ready to implement your plan when needed. It might play out like this: Jeremy comes in late to your class with bloodshot eyes, a pale complexion, a sheepish grin, and an identifiable odor. He slides into his seat. You notice the muffled laughter from  his friends as he tries to get settled. You engage him in conversation and suspect that he stopped at the "bathroom bar" on the way to class. You know it is time to implement your plan. Get your class busy doing something related to the lesson while you contact the nurse. Ideally, you can simply text and not involve any other students. Unfortunately, most teachers don't have ready access to a phone. If you don't have access to a phone, you can write a note, enclose it in a sealed envelope, and ask a trusted student or another teacher to run the note for you. Then you can resume teaching your class, and Jeremy will be called out without knowing that you set it up. This is a way for Jeremy to get help and for you to maintain control in your classroom.

If you have seen the movie *Finding Nemo*, you will remember that Nemo had one undeveloped fin, and his father was afraid that

Nemo wouldn't be able to keep up with the other fish. You will have some Nemos in your classroom.

Nemo Zoe

Zoe has multiple sclerosis and is strapped to a wheelchair because she doesn't have control of her muscles. She has a computer that speaks for her. She operates it by hitting her ear on a control to maneuver the mouse. She comes to class with a staff aide.

Classroom Strategies: Always remember that inside each student is a soul with a full range of emotions and needs and a brain that can be as sharp as all the others in your classroom. To the best of your ability, include these children in all of your classroom activities. Spend some one-on-one time with your special students so you understand their limitations and know how they want to be treated. Sometimes, it is helpful to educate your class about certain physical limitations. For instance, in Zoe's case, the students might be much more empathetic and welcoming with an understanding of the condition. It is necessary to get the afflicted person's approval before you use this approach; often, he/she is more than willing to do the educating. In the following snapshot, Brock's story illustrates this point.

 **Student Snapshot**

Brock joined our class as a student aide. He was an energetic, engaging, optimistic senior. He was a well-known person around school, not only because of his energy and personality, but also because he negotiated the entire building, steps and all, on two prostheses. He did not use canes or a walker. Both

of Brock's legs had been amputated at his upper thigh as an infant because of a birth defect. He told his story to our ninth and tenth graders and answered all of their questions about how he was able to live with his handicap. His grand finale was doing a handstand on the table and exhibiting how he walked on his hands when he wasn't wearing his legs. Not only did the students learn that it is okay to ask questions and learn about the afflictions of others, but they came to love and admire Brock for the person he was and no longer were curious about why he walked with a strange gait.

Nemo Brian

Brian has a withered arm that he hides inside his sleeve. He doesn't want the other kids to notice. He has been teased too often. He gets frustrated when his math teacher expects him to use a compass because he can't hold the paper with one hand and use the compass with the other. He just puts his head down and pretends to feel sick.

Always consider whether a student like Brian can easily do the classroom activity. When two hands are necessary, modify the assignment, or ask the student privately how you can help. Try the assignment yourself with only one arm to see if you can do it.

Nemo Amy

When you call on Amy to read a paragraph aloud, she sounds like a competent reader, but when you ask her a question about what she just read, you realize she doesn't have a clue.

Amy may have a learning disorder. Make sure that you include several instructional modes in your lesson plans. Remember, some students will learn from reading, some from listening, and some from engaging in hands-on activities. Most students need all three modes to learn and remember new material. There could be others in your class with diagnosed or undiagnosed learning disorders. Often, schools schedule "a class within a class" for these students, meaning a special education teacher is assigned to your classroom to help these students. Don't be intimidated if your schedule includes a "class within a class" because you will probably learn very quickly that you enjoy having the second teacher in the room. If you suspect that a student has a learning disability, you should bring it to the attention of the special-education department.

Watch Out for Predators

"Watch your step; everybody else does!" Anonymous

While you are busy trying to be everything to everybody, you don't want to let down your guard. There are always a few students out to challenge you.

Hatchet Fish

Caleb slides into his seat ten seconds after the bell rings. You give him the tardy and inform him that he owes you fifteen minutes after school. He gets irate and says that you are picking on him. On his way out of the classroom, he says that he is going to tell his dad how unfair you are. His dad is on the school board.

Classroom Strategies: You have to remain fair and consistent. You can't show favoritism. Have faith that the administration will support you. Keep good records so you can back up your actions.

Viper Fish

Valorie is a beautiful sixteen-year-old girl who sits in the front row. She laughs at your jokes and flirts with you. She likes to linger after class to ask you questions. You are sure she has a crush on you.

Classroom Strategies: Male and female students can and do develop crushes on their teachers. You, as the teacher, must always maintain a professional demeanor. For example, keep your door open when working alone with a student. If you are concerned about being alone with a student, then meet him/her in a more public place, such as the school library. Certainly, no matter your intentions, allowing students to drop in at your home for a social visit is loaded with inherent dangers and risks. You must avoid any and all behaviors that might appear inappropriate.

Keep in mind that most students who want to get closer to teachers are not predators. In this day and age, when some family situations are less than desirable, it is not uncommon for young people to turn to a teacher. Teachers, caring and compassionate by nature, are inclined to provide support. Sometimes, the magnitude of the problem requires training that a classroom teacher does not have. You can best assist some students by guiding them to the help they need. Become familiar with the social services in your area. Refer the needy student to the school counselor when appropriate. Do not get emotionally hooked.

Some teachers have failed to draw the line between compassion and other less appropriate emotions. Unfortunately, they have crossed the line, lost their jobs, and even been prosecuted for their actions. Don't let the lines get fuzzy between teacher and student. While adolescents have adult bodies, their emotions are still immature. Whether the student is a predator or just someone in need, you are the adult, and he/she is a child. At all times, remember that inappropriate actions, real or imagined, can put your career in jeopardy and even lead to you being charged as a pedophile.

Watch out for the average joes, smarty pants, tuned outs, bullheads, darters, flounders, solos, grass carp, and nemos. Because you will have many different types of fish in your bowl, it is your duty to see that every single fish is healthy and thriving. You must be vigilant in keeping the water fresh and clean, the environment safe and functional, and the food healthy and plentiful. You must also know your limits and know when to seek help. Finally, you must watch out for the predators, like the hatchet fish and viper fish, who can threaten your career and your peace of mind.

The Reflection Pool

Can you identify any of the fish that were discussed in this chapter from your earlier classroom experiences? Reflect now on the students you were thinking about while you were reading, and jot down some ideas on how you plan to help these types of students achieve success in your classroom.

Chapter Seven

Sink or Swim

Key Topics:
- **Establishing Order in the Fishbowl**
- **What to Do When the Bobber Goes Under**
- **Do Not Let the Way-Below-the-Line Behaviors Sink You**

Establishing Order in the Fishbowl

Do you know what to do when the clown fish acts up? When the blowfish starts blowing bubbles? When the zebra fish play in the flow of other fish? When the big-mouthed bass continues to talk? When the sharks try to intimidate others? When the octopus cannot keep his hands to himself? You need to civilize the fishbowl by establishing and maintaining order. You must incorporate your personal style into any guidelines you develop. Thus, it will be helpful for you to visualize and describe in words the ideal learning environment. Remember, your description does not have to be like the classic, textbook definitions you read in college.

EXERCISE: What are the characteristics of an orderly classroom?

_____

_____

_____

_____

_____

_____

_____

_____

_____

_____

Now, with your description in hand, how do you create your perfect classroom? It seems logical that you will establish guidelines, and the students will follow them. This may work well for Attila the Hun, but it probably will not work for you.

There are all kinds of teachers and many ways to approach classroom discipline. Some instructors have rules posted around the room. This assures that students know the guidelines and precludes their pleading ignorance when confronted with inappropriate behavior. Others have no posted rules, but things go well because the students know what is expected of them. Some teachers involve the students in defining the norms by which they are willing to abide. (See T.Box: Discipline Resources.)

Whatever method you choose, be aware; almost any rule ultimately leads to the same important goal: respect for one another.

 **Teacher Snapshot**

With the advent of the ninety-minute class period, all teachers had one AAP (academic advisement period), a sort of homeroom/study hall where the teacher was responsible for the students and their behavior—not an easy situation for a teacher. Students were to study, do homework, and make up missed class work and tests. They were allowed to move to other classrooms, the office, the counselor, or the nurse with an appropriate pass. Of course, some students never had any homework and just seemed to enjoy being disruptive.

Marjorie Russell set her AAP class on the right track on the first day of school. As students approached, they could hear the rockin' beat of "Respect" by Aretha Franklin wafting out of the room. Ms. Russell then welcomed everyone warmly and proceeded to lead a discussion on what respect was and how one did and did not show it toward teachers and peers alike. That was a very positive, fun way to let young people know the boundaries without alienating them. Students loved being in her AAP and behaved well, for the most part, from the beginning.

The golden rule is to treat others as you want to be treated. This rule is very true for the teacher as well as the students. Treating people with respect helps them to feel important and successful. It will enable the students to develop healthy self-images and feel that their contributions are valued. Students who feel good and believe they can learn and perform at expected levels will interact well with others. This can also be true for students who resemble sharks or piranhas, if handled properly. (See T.Box: Activities for Classroom Environment.)

"What kids need today is plenty of LSD—love, security, and discipline." — Anonymous

EXERCISE: *Reflect on your ideal, orderly classroom. What rules or norms will you need? What code of conduct will be necessary? Write down your expectations for classroom conduct.*

_____

_____

_____

_____

_____

_____

_____

What to Do When the Bobber Goes Under

After you have established your code of conduct, some fish will test the water. Think in terms of "below the waterline" behaviors, behaviors that cross the line and constitute serious offenses. Establish the below-the-line behaviors,

and then preplan what you will do to deal with these behaviors. Being proactive will eliminate reactive behavior on your part. A little advance planning will give you confidence and will result in creative solutions.

Student Snapshot

Susan was a very bright, popular honor student and was actively involved in several school activities. Additionally, she was a talented ice skater and spent many hours after school at the local rink. Ms. Hardesty was shocked and dismayed when she caught Susan with a cheat sheet during a test. Following her standard procedure, she took the slip of paper from Susan's hand, removed the test, and stapled the cheat sheet to the test. Ms. Hardesty then explained to Susan that after school she should tell her parents what had happened, because her teacher would be calling that evening to speak with them.

That evening, Susan's father took the call. He explained that he and his wife were in the middle of a divorce, and he apologized for his daughter's behavior. He said Susan was stressed and had "too much on her plate." He did not excuse her behavior, however, and accepted Ms. Hardesty's explanation that Susan would receive a zero on that test, which would be averaged in with all her other grades. He promised there would be no more such behavior from Susan.

Ms. Hardesty greeted Susan the next day with a smile and treated her no differently than usual. That young lady worked so hard until the end of the school year that she earned an A in the class after all. Sometimes, unfortunate incidents can have positive outcomes.

There will always be cheaters in the classroom. Actually, many students think it is perfectly okay to cheat as long as they don't get caught. Honor students can be the worst offenders because they need the grades to get into their choice schools. They know others cheat, and they want to keep a competitive edge. Assume that students will cheat. Decide how you will handle cheaters, and share that information with your classes at the beginning of the year. Be consistent, and treat all students the same no matter how popular they are or who their parents are. Be proactive. Make up two or three different versions of the same test and distribute them so students can't cheat off each other. Require your students to run their research papers through a Web site like www.turnitin.com, which highlights in red print anything in the paper that has been plagiarized from the Internet. Make them staple the printout from this Web site to their original paper before they turn it in. Watch for students who try to send electronic text messages with cell phones or cheat from crib notes on calculators. Don't give fill-in-the-blank worksheets on chapters unless you are okay with students copying each other's papers. You might want to reconsider those worksheets all together, because students don't read the chapter; they only find the boldface key phrases. Is this the level of learning you were hoping for? Make it clear that you won't tolerate cheating, and stick to it.

Some negative behaviors can be labeled "way below the waterline," while others simply cause a ripple in the classroom flow. You must deal with both kinds of negative behavior, but the majority of the misbehaviors you will encounter will be ripples.

They seem small, but if not squelched, they could strengthen into whitecaps, and soon you will find yourself in a real mess.

Examples of ripples, with solutions, include the following:

- A student does not work on the assignment and loudly yawns, indicating that he thinks it is boring. *Take the student aside to talk and find out what is going on. Ask why the work is not done. Explain what this is doing to the student's grade and how disruption affects the rest of the class. Devise a plan that will help the student complete the assignments. Be caring and sensitive to the possibility that a personal problem is interfering with the student's focus. If this is the case, encourage the student to see the school counselor. Offer to go along for support.*
- A student calls another student an inappropriate name. *Stop it right then. Discuss with the students what respect for one another means. Refer to your classroom norms. Let them know there are appropriate ways to disagree with someone. Although forcing an apology from the offending student is not an effective way of dealing with the situation, some closure must be reached rapidly. Ask the students involved if they want to settle it now or if they prefer to go to the office for mediation. Usually, students will appreciate the chance to avoid the office, and apologies will be exchanged. Then, drop the matter, and go on with class.*
- A number of students are talking while you give directions for the assignment. *Stop talking, and wait quietly until they realize you are watching them and waiting. After they are quiet, thank them and go on with class.*
- A student asks to go to the bathroom and comes back smelling like cigarette smoke. *You need to let the class know that you recognize what has happened and that you will not give passes for smoke breaks. You might respond by joking with the smoker, pointing out that he/she asked you for a restroom*

pass and not for a smoking pass. Tell your class that they will lose their bathroom privileges if they can't pass your "sniff test" when they return. This lets everyone know that this is not smart behavior, and they have been warned.

- A student has been tardy to your class five times during the past two weeks. *Take the student aside and visit with him/her about this problem. Perhaps he/she is coming from across campus or stopping at the restroom. Suggest ways to avoid tardies, such as by not stopping at the locker or by checking into the classroom first and then asking to go to the restroom.*

- A girl digs around in her purse and passes out chewing gum to other students during your lecture. She then continues to loudly snap her gum during the presentation. *It is best to deal with something like this right when it happens. Stop your presentation, and discuss the action and the disrespect you are feeling. If you allow gum in your classroom, tell the class that if they can't chew surreptitiously, then they will be denied the privilege. The students may have to look up the word "surreptitious," but that's education!*

Always be aware of your reaction to misbehavior. Do not react in anger. Do not let your response to the offense last longer than the behavior itself. Once the incident is over, it is over.

> *"The typical fisherman is long on optimism and short on memory." — Anonymous*

Choose consequences that will stop the offending behavior. This does not necessarily mean that you must treat all students alike. Match the consequence to the infraction and the personality of the student. If the behavior catches you off guard, and you cannot instantly invoke positive discipline measures, tell the student you will discuss the consequences for that behavior later. This not only lets you think about the right consequence but also makes the offender stew for a time, which often works to your advantage.

Make sure you can follow through with the consequences you assign. For example, don't assign five days of after-school detention if you are not willing to stay after school on those days yourself.

Often, teachers opt for a quick fix by sending the student to the office for discipline. It is important that you don't give your authority away to administrators. Teachers who frequently send students to the office appear to have limited power and authority. You want to be the lead swimmer so that you have a major influence on learning and behaviors. Dealing with your own classroom problems lets students know that you are the leader in charge of their destiny.

Don't count on your creative genius to think of appropriate consequences for disruptive behavior on the spot. It is best to plan. Brainstorm some possible behavior problems, and then match the problems to the consequence. Keep it simple—the simpler the better. You will be surprised at how writing down these things prepares you and gives you confidence for real classroom situations. Of course, you will face many unanticipated classroom situations, so you can keep adding to your list throughout the year. Live and learn.

Below you will find three sample behaviors and appropriate consequences:

- A student is late to class. Assign after-school or before-school make-up time.
- A student is visiting inappropriately. Give one warning, and then physically isolate them, removing the opportunity to socialize.
- A student is disrespectful to another student. Initiate an after-school conference including both parties. Allow the offender to see the hurt up close and acknowledge his/her responsibility for it.

Above all, be consistent and fair in your treatment of the students. Each classroom they enter may have a slightly different set of expectations, but if the teacher in charge is consistent and fair, the students can and will adjust accordingly. Remember, it is the students' perception of the classroom that matters. Remain aware that their perception of your classroom filters through you, the teacher. What you say and do and how you behave each day will leave a lasting impression on your students. Be in control of your own behaviors. Experienced teachers agree: if you respect your students, in return, they will respect you.

Be sure to review the school rules and policies so that you remain compliant. You may not agree with certain rules. Think ahead about how you will deal with students who break such rules. Otherwise, you may find yourself in a difficult situation. You do not want to be in the position of siding with the students against the administration. Make a positive effort to find out who makes the rules and when the rules are reviewed. Express interest in getting on that committee and possibly effecting change.

Do Not Let the Way-Below-the-Line Behaviors Sink You

Way-below-the-line behaviors differ from ripple behaviors in that they are serious infractions that cannot be handled within the confines of your classroom. You must refer these problems to the administrators. If students are oppositional and refuse to comply with your authority, they should be sent to the office. When students display aggressive behavior that is harmful or destructive to others, you must remove them from your classroom.

If you are worried that a student's behavior and attitude indicate the potential for a dangerous situation, talk to the principal, counselor, and parent about the inappropriate behaviors. Have a plan that you have discussed in advance with administrators for removing the student from the classroom if it becomes necessary. Then, when you send the student to the office, there will be some advance information about what has been happening. This helps put the problem in context and highlights measures you have already implemented in attempts to change the inappropriate behaviors.

"Discipline doesn't break a child's spirit half as often as the lack of it breaks a parent's heart." — Anonymous

On rare occasions, you may have a very serious and potentially dangerous problem in the classroom. Be sure to document such an incident carefully, because it might involve a criminal offense. The following real-life snapshot serves as an example of extreme, below-the-line behavior.

Student Snapshot

Joe is having a bad day. He feels aggressive and on edge. He is somewhat of a computer whiz and is most comfortable when seated at the keyboard. He normally stakes his claim on a particular machine early in the day. Today, however, he did not finish his math in time to claim one of the fifteen computers in the lab. Joe is very jealous of Harry, a somewhat quiet, reclusive student currently seated at Joe's favorite computer.

Joe approaches Harry and quietly delivers a verbal threat: "Get off my computer, or I'll get you!"

Harry, for once, asserts himself and replies, "I was here first, so this is my machine."

> *Joe erupts in anger and pulls out an X-acto knife he swiped from art class. He impulsively stabs Harry in the thigh. Chaos reigns in the computer lab, and the teacher has to deal with it.*

Planning or conferencing could not have preceded this difficult time in the classroom. So, have a plan for handling the unexpected, severe classroom problems. Remove the offending student or students as quickly as possible to the principal's office. If the student is unwilling to leave, contact the principal to come and remove the student; or, if all else fails, remove yourself and the other students to a safe place and send a trustworthy student to the office for assistance. Do not leave the students in your charge unsupervised. Ask teachers close by for assistance if needed. Most of all, become familiar with and follow the policies and procedures at your school for dealing with severe discipline problems.

Even a perfect teacher cannot foresee how any one student will behave in any given moment. In extreme circumstances such as these, you should receive total support from the administration. In fact, trying to handle these behaviors on your own could jeopardize your job. Rules will be in place to cover such occurrences, and you and your principal can make decisions according to school policy. Never try to handle way-below-the-line behaviors on your own, unless you have no other choice.

 ## Teacher Snapshot

> *Emily, a first-year teacher, had been experiencing difficulties with many of the students in her fifth-grade class. Several were learning disabled, many were exhibiting bad behavior, and a few were downright mean. She had been discussing the problem with the principal and trying to learn from more experienced teachers how to cope with the kids.*

One day, a girl in class got so angry that she threw a chair. Emily immediately sent a trusted student to the office to get the principal and made sure the other children were safe, while keeping a close eye on the enraged youngster. The student sent to summon help returned with this message: "Principal Henry is out of the building. Mrs. James is in charge, but she said she couldn't come right now because she is eating lunch." Emily was appalled. She wondered why she had ever wanted to teach.

What can a teacher do when the administration is not supportive? This situation is what nightmares are made of. In all fairness, administrators are sometimes overwhelmed with minor classroom problems and feel the teachers should be able to handle these things themselves. In some cases, they are right on target. A good teacher does not rely on the principal for day-to-day, trivial classroom difficulties. A teacher who manages classroom discipline with forethought and fairness will gain the respect of the students and eventually have few problems. The throwing of a chair, however, is not a minor problem. Because no help was forthcoming, Emily dealt with the problem herself. She isolated the offending student and asked another teacher to watch her students while she escorted the angry girl to the office. The student sat with the secretary until someone could talk to her, and Emily returned to her classroom and relieved the teacher who watched her students. Using her skills and ingenuity, Emily was able to defuse a situation when administrative support seemed to be lacking. Class resumed, and she was able to address the issue at a more appropriate time.

EXERCISE: Given the following list of inappropriate classroom behaviors, first identify each as a way-below-the-line behavior or simply as a negative ripple. Next, determine which behavior expectation has not been upheld. Last, list consequences you believe are appropriate.

1. *A young lady is painting her nails during your lecture.*

   _____
   _____
   _____
   _____

2. *Two boys get into an altercation in class. One has the other in a headlock.*

   _____
   _____
   _____
   _____

3. *You are giving directions for an upcoming classroom activity. You hear giggling in the classroom, but you are unsure where it is coming from. Students are generally distracted.*

   _____
   _____
   _____
   _____

4. *A student comes to school obviously distressed and out of sorts. Although normally a good student, she cannot seem to pay attention and has disrupted class with wise remarks twice already.*

   _____
   _____
   _____
   _____

This is the way we see these behaviors and how we might deal with them.

- Negative ripple—Disruptive behavior shows lack of respect for you and other students. Invite the student to stay after school and have her paint something that needs it, maybe a bookshelf or bulletin board trim.
- Below-the-line behavior—School rules state no fighting. Send a trustworthy student to the office to get the principal or call on the intercom. Ask another student to get the teacher next door. Move other students out of the way to safety. Reasoning and the presence of the principal or another teacher will likely cause the fighters to break it up. Separate them, and allow them a minute to calm down. Be sure an adult escorts them to the office.
- Negative ripple—Students are displaying a lack of respect for your presentation. Become absolutely silent. Wait for the giggling to stop, and then use an "I" statement: "I feel very frustrated when you giggle while I am trying to give you directions, because to do this activity and really enjoy it, you need those directions. I want you to notice that we have wasted two minutes on this. You will all remain two minutes after the bell rings before you are dismissed for lunch today." Then continue class.
- Negative ripple—This does show a lack of respect for you and others, but because it is out of character, the behavior should be a red flag for you. The student may be crying for help. Ask the student to step into the hall with you. Say, "I'm worried about your disruptive behavior because it is not like you to act up. Are you all right? Do you have a problem I could help you with?" Genuine concern will probably illicit an apology and maybe even a disclosure of a greater personal problem. Be caring and supportive. Ask if the student wants to visit a counselor.

If the student shows a desire to continue with class and promises to behave, then just continue with class. Confer with the student later to assure yourself that she is feeling better.

The Reflection Pool

What is your greatest weakness as far as classroom discipline is concerned? What do you fear most that might occur in your classroom? How might you plan to deal with the situation?

Chapter Eight
Casting for Positive Parents

Key Topics:
- **Be a Good Angler**
- **Proper Equipment, Accurate Cast, and Appropriate Bait**
- **Landing Tricky Fish**

Be a Good Angler

A good angler catches many fish by working with familiar, well-cared-for equipment, and by paying attention to detail. He uses appetizing bait and accurate casts with the proper follow-through. Similarly, teachers catch positive parents by establishing caring relationships with their students, and knowing good classroom-management techniques. They use the right bait, make an accurate cast when defining a problem, and have a nice follow-through.

"The one thing children wear out faster than shoes is parents." — John J. Plomp

Almost all parents want the best for their children. Some may not parent well, but they do care. Many parents think they know a lot about schooling because they have experienced it, and sometimes it was not the best experience. Therefore, some parents tend to judge teachers and side with their kids, despite the circumstances.

 **Parent Snapshot**

A teacher caught a student cheating and became involved in a lengthy, controversial conference with the parents. Finally, in desperation, the parents confronted the teacher, saying, "If you were a better teacher, my kid wouldn't have to cheat to get the grade she deserves!"

Protective parents with negative attitudes about school make teachers reluctant to interact with them. Nevertheless, experience shows that most parents will be helpful if given the chance to become a partner in setting educational goals—especially if they can tell that you care and want the best school experience for their child. Therefore, contacting parents regularly is important.

Never underestimate the power of a phone call. If you call parents early in the year with a positive message, then communication later in the year may be greatly facilitated. Usually, the parents of bright, obedient, cheerful students welcome a phone call from a teacher. Parents of students who struggle with schoolwork, behavior,  manners, and attitude are the ones you especially need to contact. As early as possible, identify those students who may need special attention, and then call their parents just to say something pleasant about the students before they have time to get into trouble. This will establish a relationship with those parents, who may be more willing to listen to you later if difficulties arise.

A parent/teacher conference does not have to be a negative experience for either party. Before any interaction, try to put yourself in the parents' place. The parents are coming to see you to discuss their child, who is an extension of themselves. When you criticize the child, you are also criticizing the parents, who may be apprehensive and defensive. Remember to be aware of the parents' egos, because coming to school can bring out their child state and result in confrontation (see chapter two for a review). You need to take control of this interaction and stay in your adult ego state. If the parents have initiated the contact, and you are unsure of the underlying motivation, look on the conference as an opportunity to understand your student better and try to remain as positive and caring as possible.

Simple suggestions are provided in the next two sections to help you facilitate positive and productive conference experiences.

Proper Equipment, Accurate Cast, and Appropriate Bait

> *"The real art of conversation is not only to say the right thing at the right place but to leave unsaid the wrong thing at the tempting moment." — Dorothy Nevill*

During your initial contact with parents, be sure to start out with something sincere and positive about the child: "I enjoy your son so much because ...." If they believe you really care and do see the good things, then they will be more open, honest, and accepting when discussing their child.

It is not always up to you to provide all of the solutions. Think of yourself as a facilitator, guide, and coach. This leaves you in a less combative, more respected, and powerful position. Try to use "I" messages as you approach the critical issues to diffuse some of the tension and anxiety. It will help you explain the problem openly and directly. The parent needs to know what is happening, how you feel about it, why it is a problem, and what you expect. It is good to problem-solve together because it provides an opportunity for increased understanding and may result in improved student behavior.

Always be aware of the current dominant ego state of the parent: parent, child, or adult. If the parent is in the adult state, you are in luck; if you remain in your adult state and approach the issue from an objective viewpoint, then things should go well. If you observe that the parent has come to talk in the throes of a parent or child ego state, be a reflective listener. Listen carefully to the parent's message and paraphrase it in your response after acknowledging how you think the person is feeling. Hopefully, the parent's adult ego will emerge when you recognize the feelings elicited by the parent or child state.

For a parent conference to be productive, you must convince the parents that you have their student's best interests at heart. You will not accomplish this by expressing your disappointment with their child in a mean and spiteful way. Do not let your frustrations boil over into vindictive tattling. Try to be generous but factual in your assessment of the situation. Remain calm, collected, and caring. If the child is a hellion with many faults, try focusing on only one or two behaviors you want to change. Do not overwhelm the parent with a litany of sins. Try to balance every negative thing you need to say about a child with something positive. Think of a sandwich—positive, negative, positive.

Most parents realize their children are not angels. If you approach a problem in an open, caring way, then parents often will share similar behaviors and situations they face at home with their child and be receptive to formulating solutions with or accepting guidance from you. Remember, if you alienate the parents, then the problem in the classroom is not solved, and things will only get worse.

The following is an example to help you brush up on a casting technique that requires the proper bait choice to hook parents into becoming your allies in solving classroom problems.

Student Snapshot

Johnny has a very difficult time paying attention in class. He tends to be the class clown and does not take his studies seriously. He talks to others, is loud, and has a hard time sitting still. He is quite bright and picks up the lessons easily, but he interferes so much that others cannot learn. He rarely has the patience to complete assigned class work and never does his homework. Thus, he is not passing the class, even though he usually passes the tests. You have visited with Johnny about these problems and have seen little or no change in behavior. You set up a parent conference for tomorrow.

You need to do some homework before the meeting by developing a plan of action:

STEP 1. Brainstorm all the negative things that you feel need to be addressed. Go ahead ... put them all down. No one but you will see this list. Your list might look something like this:

Johnny is ...

1. Disruptive
2. Frustrating
3. Not doing class work well
4. Talkative
5. Disrespectful (will not correct behaviors when asked)
6. Loud
7. Not doing any homework
8. Rude and mouthy
9. A pain!

"Your least favorite student probably has a least favorite teacher." — Todd Whitaker

STEP 2. *Make a list of positives for Johnny. Be generous; it's okay to stretch reality. Try to put a positive spin on each negative trait you have cited. Your list might look like this:*

Johnny is …
1. Clever (might be a stand-up comic someday)
2. Fun to work with … full of surprises
3. Able to start out well on class work
4. Able to get along well with others
5. Not verbally disrespectful (says he will try but does not follow through)
6. Not shy or timid
7. Probably very busy at home as he does not do homework
8. Not afraid to express what he is thinking
9. Able to learn and pass tests

STEP 3. *Condense and prioritize the negative list into a shorter, more concise one, and eliminate those items that reflect how you feel. For example, negative behaviors 1, 4, 6, and 8 might all be classified under "disruptive." Behaviors 3, 5, and 7 might be condensed to "lack of effort to change." Numbers 2 and 9 are oriented toward how you feel. They are not relevant; eliminate them. Now, our list looks much better. Pick the one or two behaviors you want to change:*

1. Johnny is disruptive.
2. Johnny is unable or unwilling to change bad habits (behavior and work).

STEP 4. *Design your "I" message, and preface it with a positive statement. Here are two possible messages:*

"Johnny is so clever; I'm sure he'll be a stand-up

comic someday, but <u>I feel</u> I cannot teach my class appropriately <u>when he</u> disrupts with joking and talking <u>because</u> other students cannot learn in that environment. <u>I want</u> Johnny to be quiet and attentive during class presentations."

"Johnny is very bright. I know he is learning because he usually passes his tests, but <u>I feel</u> he will not succeed in this class <u>if he</u> continues to turn in incomplete class work and no homework. I must give him zeros for all that work, and when averaged with his test scores, this will result in a failing grade. <u>I want</u> him to change his behavior, stay on task, and do his homework. I want his grade to reflect what he really has learned. I know you want Johnny to be successful, and so do I."

STEP 5. *Brainstorm some suggestions to help Johnny improve. Again, make a list:*

1. Move him away from others.
2. Give him classroom-management jobs to keep him active and involved.
3. Make a written contract with him to focus him on the changes he needs to make.
4. After he understands a concept, let him move away from the others and complete his class work in a quiet place.
5. Send the parents a weekly written progress report to sign and return to the school.
6. Ask the parents to reduce privileges (i.e., TV, music, phone, friends) until after homework is completed.

7. To provide an outlet for his showmanship, allow Johnny to get up in front of the class and explain a key concept to the class.
8. Write up a discipline referral for Johnny to the principal. (See T.Box: Helpful Forms.)

STEP 6. Implement the plan. It is time to land that fish and become a parent/teacher team. During the conference, remember to employ reflective listening, and be alert to which ego state the parents have brought to the table. Be flexible, voice positives, and visit in a comfortable, friendly manner. Explain the problem as you have planned, incorporating your positive statements into your "I" message. Talk to the parents about whether or not the same behaviors occur at home and about what they think is happening. How do they handle this at home? Does it work? Share some of your ideas and suggestions to effect change. Ask what the parents think would work best and solicit additional suggestions. Make a plan, and together discuss it with Johnny. Leave the parents on a positive note; smile, shake hands, and assure them you look forward to working in partnership with them in the future.

Be sure to keep in touch with Johnny's parents. Remember to include positives when sending notes home, making short phone calls, or e-mailing. If Johnny has an especially poor day, remind him to tell his parents, as you will be calling that evening. Remember, parents are allies, not opponents. We all want the same thing, a positive learning experience for this young person.

"Coming together is a beginning; keeping together is progress; working together is success." — Henry Ford

Landing Tricky Fish

The prior example was written assuming the conference was being held for a difficult student with involved parents. Parents come in many different varieties, not all of them easy to deal with.

 Teacher Snapshot

A young man was sent to the vice-principal's office because he was disrupting class. It was discovered that he had not taken his morning medication that was necessary for him to maintain focus. The vice-principal called the parent and asked that the parent bring the medication or come to school to take her son home. The parent replied that she did not have the money to refill the prescription. Since the student received many services including free medication, this was puzzling to the administrator. Once again the vice-principal stated that the parent would need to either bring the medication or pick up her son and keep him home until he had his medication. The parent replied, "You are interrupting me. You are supposed to keep him during the day. This is the time I take my bubble bath, so you will need to keep him."

What happens when the child is struggling and the parents are oppositional, overly-involved, or uninvolved?

Oppositional parents blame you for whatever their child does and stands up for the child even if he/she is absolutely in the wrong. These parents can become loud and abusive, and frequently they embarrass their children. Trying to visit with them on your own may be a losing battle. Instead, set up a conference including the counselor or principal. This way, there are no misunderstandings concerning what has occurred.

Helicopter parents, those that hover continually, are overly concerned about their child's progress. These parents are very helpful as grade-school volunteers, but as their children enter junior high and high school, their involvement might become intrusive. Most teenagers are embarrassed if their parents are always around. Helicopter parents are often unrealistic about their child's grades and blame the teacher for the lack of effort or ability reflected by the grade. For example, many students will consciously work hard

enough to get a decent grade but not work to the best of their abilities, which does not meet parental expectations. On the other hand, some students work up to their potential; yet, they do not earn grades high enough to satisfy their parents. How can these situations be resolved?

Be caring and honest, and stick to your guns. Do not raise a student's grade just to avoid controversy with hovering parents. If you need extra support, team up with your principal and school counselor to make the parents understand that their attitude might be harmful. Be thankful when you don't have a classroom full of students who have helicopter parents.

> *"The reason parents don't lead their children in the right direction is because the parents aren't going that way themselves."* — Anonymous

It is a standing joke among educators that when it comes time for school-wide parent/teacher conferences, the parents that come are not the ones the teachers need to see. That is so true. How does one deal with the invisible parent? When you have a troubled student whose parents do not show up for conferences, do not give up. Those parents may have had a poor school experience themselves and may be very uncomfortable coming to the school. Contact them individually, and try to communicate with them. Even though they may be reluctant about coming to the school, they do care about their child. After they know that you care and are trying to enlist their help in making school a positive experience for their child, they might respond in a helpful manner.

If you still have no luck and are working with junior high or high school students, then deal with the student as an adult. Hold the planned parent/teacher conference with the student alone. Have the student reflect on his/her learning progress and recognize inappropriate behaviors and the possible consequences. Often, students will respond well to this approach. If you are working with grade-school children of invisible parents, love them. Try to assume a positive adult role in their lives. These forgotten children frequently come to love school and the comfortable environment it provides. They will try to please you if they feel you really care. Sometimes, your principal or counselor might have better luck in getting these parents involved.

The Reflection Pool

Think of a child you know who would benefit from a parent/teacher conference. Prepare yourself for the conference using the steps outlined in this chapter.

Chapter Nine
Gasping for Air

Key Topics:

- **Beached**
- **Flopping in the Sand**
- **Riding the Waves**

Beached

We have all seen the film clips of the poor whale that, for one reason or another, wound up on the beach and is struggling to stay alive. If that distressed, disoriented whale had recognized that it was in trouble and had asked for help from some fellow whales, then perhaps it could have avoided the ultimate public humiliation. Unfortunately for all of us, we sometimes do not even recognize our own problems with stress until we are beached with illness, burnout, or both. The last thing we want to do is admit that we are in danger, because then others might think we are not strong and capable. After all, we are the kingfish. We thrive on stress. The weak become prey, right?

So, how do you recognize that you are on the verge of being beached by stress, and how do you avoid it? First, you need to understand what stress is and how your body responds to stress. Then, you need to learn how to be proactive in taking care of yourself and managing your stress so that you will never be beached.

When most of us think of stress, we think of worry. We think that stress is caused by negative happenings in our lives. Your body has a much broader definition of stress. Stress is anything that causes change in your life. It can be good change or bad change or even imagined change. Whether you are going on your dream vacation or going to a funeral, your body responds to it as stress. Whether you think that you might lose your job or (on the flip side) that you might get a great promotion, just imagining changes in your life brings on stress.

Some small amount of stress may be productive and can encourage us to work at a faster pace. Many of us seek out and enjoy the sensation of temporary stress, like the thrill of a roller coaster ride or the excitement of a new romance. A little bit of stress can be a positive thing.

Think of all the changes in just one day at school that can affect your stress level. Imagine yourself brushing your teeth and, at the same time, organizing your day in your mind when the phone rings. It is your mother. She talks nonstop for fifteen minutes. You look at the clock and realize that you only have forty-five minutes before the first bell rings at school, and you are not dressed. You frantically get dressed and jump into your car. You step into the building just in time, but not before the principal sees you walk through the door and looks at his watch without saying a word. You start your morning routine with your class, and then the school's alarm goes off. Oh, no—you forgot that there was a drill today, and you can't remember if this alarm signals fire or tornado. Should you get your kids out of the building or down in the basement? As you return from the fire drill, you trip on the step and twist your ankle. Another teacher steps in to help and sends a student to get the nurse. You are embarrassed as you sit on the step while waiting for a wheelchair. You are pleasantly surprised, however, that your students seem concerned, which makes you feel better. You worry about your lack of lesson plans and worksheets for the substitute teacher because you didn't arrive early this morning as you had planned to get your activities ready. You suspect this will all be noted on your performance evaluation slated for review tomorrow. Should you just hand in your resignation now?

You can see how any change, real or imagined, can cause stress on the body and affect your emotional well-being. For major changes in your life like getting married or divorced, moving, or losing a loved one, the effects can carry over for long periods, as long as a year or more. (See T.Box: Stress Tests.)

When the body is overstressed, physical damage can result in several areas. Overstress can cause fatigue, aches and pains, crying spells, depression, anxiety attacks, and sleep disturbances. Ulcers, cramps and diarrhea, colitis, and irritable bowel problems can result. High levels of stress can also contribute to thyroid gland malfunction, high blood pressure, heart attacks, abnormal heartbeat, strokes, decreased resistance to infections, and itchy skin rashes. Sounds awful, doesn't it? The truth is, stress causes a multitude of our physical and mental problems.[12]

Try to become aware of stress during your daily life. Remember, it can come from a variety of sources and too much might become dangerous.

> *"Many people suffer poor health, not because of what they eat, but from what is eating them."* — *Anonymous*

Flopping in the Sand

 Teacher Snapshot

When a debate coach first started taking students to tournaments, his school asked him to be the driver on the minibus to save money. The coach started having problems with diarrhea and went to the doctor about it. The wise doctor asked if the teacher felt especially stressed about anything. Soon, the coach was telling the doctor that he didn't like the responsibility of driving the students in the bus. He often thought about what could happen if he became distracted. After this visit to the doctor, the coach went to his principal and said that if they

wanted him to participate in tournaments, then the school would have to provide a driver. The school provided a driver, and that was the end of the problem with diarrhea.

You need to recognize the signs of stress before you find yourself flopping around in the sand, gasping for breath. If you are aware of the red flags of overstress and are proactive in taking care of yourself, then you will be able to stay in the water and swim with the big fish.

The first thing you need to do to manage stress is to recognize the signs of it. If you begin to experience any of these symptoms, realize that you could be heading for shore if you don't take immediate action.

Signs of Stress[13]

- Feeling tired and anxious most of the time
- Getting angry or irritated more often or more quickly than you used to
- Having problems sleeping or wanting to sleep too much
- Worrying about work dominates your thoughts
- Getting sick more often
- Overeating or not eating enough
- Having trouble with concentration
- Feeling overwhelmed

EXERCISE: *Make a list of the things that stress you. What symptoms of stress do you read in your body?*

_____

_____

_____

_____

_____

_____

_____

_____

_____

_____

Some people have personalities that make them more prone to develop stress-related illnesses. Look at the following list. If these traits describe you, you know that you are vulnerable to the ravages of stress and need to be vigilant in taking care of yourself.

Stress-Prone Personality Traits[14]

- You have more to do than the time that you have allows.
- You take multitasking to a whole new level.
- Hurry is your middle name.
- You have no patience and are easily frustrated.
- You don't know how to relax.
- You always want to win and be better than everyone else.

EXERCISE: *Which personality traits listed above do you see in yourself? Just being aware of these traits can help you to guard against them.*

_____
_____
_____
_____
_____
_____
_____
_____
_____

Riding the Waves

Stress is a part of life. In order to survive the shark-infested waters, you must learn to take control of stress before it takes control of you. There are many things that you can do to help reduce and manage the inevitable stresses in your life:

Ways to Take Care of Stress[15]

- **Be proactive rather than reactive.** If an important event is coming up, plan. When you are unsure about how you should do a task, go to the experts and get educated. Adhering to the Boy Scout motto, "Be prepared," will help you immensely in managing your stress level.
- **Prioritize.** When you feel like you have a hundred things to do at once, and your mind is racing, trying to remember everything, make a list. Then, organize the list into what must be done immediately and what can wait. Be realistic. How many things on that list are your "should dos" rather than "have to dos?"
- **Work to change what needs to be changed, and learn to accept the things that you cannot change.** You will be wasting your time and energy swimming in circles if you try to change things that are out of your control. If the unfriendly, supercritical veteran teacher across the hall is always rubbing you the wrong way, you will not be able to change the personality of that teacher. What you can control is how you respond to him. You can choose to let this person upset you each day, or you can choose to ignore him and not let him have any of your energy. The way you see the world and the way he sees the world are very different. You do not have to enter into his sphere.

EXERCISE: What have you done to reduce and manage the stress levels in your life?

_____

_____

_____

_____

_____

_____

_____

_____

"Good health just doesn't take care of itself, and it is most often lost by assuming it will." — Anonymous

Because stress, both good and bad, will always be a part of your life, you need to learn how to take good care of yourself, both physically and mentally, in order to maintain a healthy, balanced lifestyle. The following ideas will help you keep stress at a manageable level and allow you to enjoy your life both at school and at home.

Strategies for Maintaining a Balanced Life[16]

- **Exercise** on a regular basis. Walking, jogging, weight lifting, pilates, yoga, or whatever appeals to you—just do something each day.
- **Sleep.** Lack of sleep is one of the most common causes of stress.
- **Eat healthy.** Limit your intake of caffeine, alcohol, refined sugar, and salt. Increase the amount of low-fat, high-fiber foods you eat. If you suffer from panic attacks, you should know that caffeine can trigger an attack.
- **Talk to someone regularly.** Don't keep feelings inside. At the end of the day, you need to debrief. Just like police officers, firefighters, and paramedics, teachers need to talk about their day so they can let it go and relax.
- **Attend to your spiritual self.** Take time to meditate, pray, self-reflect, read inspirational writings, or watch inspirational movies or shows.

- **Take a break from news.** If you are a news junkie and are always tuned into the happenings of the world, sometimes it is a good idea to take a break. When you allow yourself to be continuously bombarded with the atrocities and the negativity that are reported 24/7, you add significantly to the stress in your life. Remember, you have little or no control of much that is happening outside of your little world, so keep it in perspective.
- **Forgive others.** Forgiving someone does not mean giving permission to that person to repeat the offensive behavior. It does not mean that the behavior was acceptable. It means that you are going to let the matter go and not drag angry, resentful feelings through your day or through your life. Think about who is being hurt by your unwillingness to forgive. Is it only you? Why allow negative feelings to take up so much of your energy? You have control over your thoughts, and your thoughts affect your emotional responses; negative thoughts lead to negative feelings. We choose whether or not to take offense in the first place. Let go of the anger. Try to see the situation from the other's point of view, or just decide that you will not allow the other person to dominate your thoughts and feelings.
- **Eliminate toxic people from your life.** If someone in your life always ruins your day, avoid that person. Of course, if that person happens to be your principal or a student, then you will have to learn to get along without letting him/her get to you.
- **Don't assume anything you hear to be true without clarification.** An extreme amount of emotional energy can be expended on an assumption. The school community is just like any other working group. Gossip is rampant. Don't allow yourself to be stressed or to risk looking foolish because you chose to react to an assumption.
- **Don't take things personally.** Other people's opinions

are all about them and their likes and dislikes; they are not really about you. When someone compliments you on the color of your shirt, they are saying that the color is one of their favorites, not that you are a great person because you are wearing that color.

- **Make time for the things that you enjoy.**
- **Have fun and play!**
- **Get plenty of laughs.**
- **Get a pet.**
- **Soothe the senses with music and color.**

EXERCISE: What have you done to maintain balance in your life?

Take care of yourself; nobody else is going to do that for you. To enjoy your life, you have to be able to ride the waves.

The Reflection Pool

Name one person or situation that is presently causing additional stress in your life. Name three things that you could do to reduce or eliminate this stress. What are some lifestyle changes you could make to help you manage stress more effectively?

Chapter Ten
Angling for a Career

Key Topics:
- Teaching Is a Tough Job
- Find Your Niche
- You May Need Bifocal Goggles

Teaching Is a Tough Job

 ### *Teacher Snapshot*

Georgia Thompson's first teaching job was at a middle school in Daly City, California, in 1961. The neighborhood was rough, and the kids were tough. She was expected to teach four different math classes within her one classroom, ranging from basic math to algebra. It was a difficult job, but not one that she was afraid to tackle. Georgia knew that she could teach, but she was not prepared for the student behavior and the lack of administrative support. She had to confiscate knives that the girls would hide in their beehive hairstyles. It was not unusual for her students to miss school because they were arrested the night before.

She remembers her anger at and frustration with the school administration over a particular incident when she sent a girl to the office for cussing her out in front of the entire class. The girl was returned to class with not even a reprimand because she was a "troubled child." At that point, Georgia felt she had lost all credibility with her students.

The one bright spot in the year was the time she spent with the kids after school. Students who really wanted to succeed talked comfortably with her about the problems they faced. Georgia never returned to teaching after that first year. She did go back to college to become a certified counselor and established a very successful private practice. Although her talents were not lost to society, they were certainly lost to the educational system. What a shame.

Teaching is a tough job, and it is getting tougher every day. It is important to be realistic about your chosen profession, to analyze your training and skills, and to know yourself well enough to see how you fit into the big picture.

> *"The school kids in some towns are getting so tough that teachers are playing hooky."* — E. C. McKenzie

Our educational system is now facing a workforce crisis. The pool of experienced teachers with twenty-plus years is rapidly declining. Each year, more experienced teachers join the ranks of the retired. Sadly, statistics show that on average, a third of newly hired teachers leave during their first three years; almost half leave during their first five years.[17]

Why does this happen? Some of our new teachers have poorly stocked tackle boxes. They do not have the essential skills and knowledge to survive the treacherous waters. Some adults find today's youth so complex and difficult to work with that they perceive teaching as a nearly impossible job. Others deplore the low pay and lack of respect found in some teaching situations. Becoming an expert teacher requires many years of experience and hard work. It requires a love of teaching, love and respect for kids, and the tenacity to stick with it even when the going gets rough. Unfortunately, many beginning teachers do not remain in the field long enough to gain that valuable experience. We fear that fine individuals who would make excellent teachers are leaving the ranks due to frustration and disillusionment. This is very sad. Assuming that experience in teaching does make a better teacher, what does this say about the quality of guidance and tutelage the children in our school systems will receive in the future?

"One reason experience is such a good teacher is that she doesn't allow any dropouts." — Anonymous

Many profess that teachers are born not made—that some people have a natural knack for teaching that others will never acquire. Others believe the art of teaching can be taught in an educational setting. They contend that most college graduates will have the foundation needed to become good teachers. Regardless of which theory you believe, there is no doubt that certain personality traits lend themselves to the teaching profession. Recall the communication information in chapter two. If you can effectively communicate with different personality types you encounter each day, then your job will seem much easier. One way to understand better if you are well suited to teaching is to complete the Assessment of Teacher Disposition. (See T.Box: Assessment of Teacher Disposition.) This useful tool will help you seriously look at your own beliefs.

"Understanding one's own magical mystery is one of the teacher's most important assets if he is to understand that everyone is thus differently equipped." — Buckminster Fuller

Another way to learn more about yourself and your students is to devote a class period to better understanding personality through color. "True Colors" is a personality test that defines personalities in terms of color, an easy and fun way to remember the differences among people. For example, gold symbolizes the person who is the rule follower. Gold people are organized and task oriented, and they want to do what is right. Blue people are caring and empathetic. They want to be helpful and to take care of others. Green folks are scientific and curious. They love to collect data and analyze it. They are not really people oriented. Orange people are artsy and flamboyant. They live for today and are easily bored. They are very creative and wonderfully uplifting, but they do not react well to structure. The True Colors material, developed by Mary Miscisin, with permission from True Colors International, the trade mark and copyright owners of "True Colors", involves fun, easy activities that let everyone discover their personality spectra. (The True Colors International website is www.true-colors.com, phone number (800) 422-4686. Mary Miscisin's website is www.PositivelyMary.com)

Of course, we all are a mixture of colors, but there is usually one that dominates. In our classes for at-risk youth, we had a high percentages of orange students. They had the hardest time adjusting to school rules and existing in the school environment. Can you imagine a gold teacher with a classroom full of orange students? (See T.Box: True Colors.)

Do you think it might be too late to look at your personal aptitude for teaching because you already have that education degree in your hand? Think about it. It is better to recognize a potential weakness now as you start your career. Otherwise, you risk getting stuck in teaching and becoming an unhappy, disgruntled grumpfish who likes young people and the job of teaching less and less each year. (We've

all had these teachers, right? You don't want to be one.) More likely than not, since you've stuck with this field through college, your instincts are good. You probably are good teacher material, and these soft diagnostic tools will simply support your career decision. If you should find your disposition and personality are not suited to teaching, never fear—you can try it and see how you feel.

We hope this book will give you the best chance possible to make it in this field. But do be aware: as an education major, you have acquired many skills that prepare you well for other kinds of work. Those young teachers who are currently leaving the field after five years are moving into a wide variety of alternative jobs. As a rule of thumb, if you accumulate five years of teaching experience, still feel uncomfortable in the job, and are not enjoying what you do, then you should reconsider your career pathway.

Find Your Niche

Let's assume you have an education degree in your hand, which means you have mastered the teaching skills and subject matter to become a successful teacher. You feel you have an adequate disposition and personality for teaching, given that you genuinely care about and enjoy helping children. You are excited to begin your new career. You recognize what an important job this is and do not expect a high salary or instant respect from others. You know you will be working extremely hard to do this job well. Congratulations—you are well on the road to making a success in this career!

"Teaching is like boxing; you win some, you lose some, but you keep going back into the ring." — Danny, Boston Public

So, what happened to all those new teachers who felt the same way you do now? Why did they give up and move on? You must realize that even though you are well-prepared academically and emotionally, this is still a very tough job. Thankfully, it gets easier as you gain experience. The best thing you can do to ensure a long, happy career in teaching is to approach the job with your eyes wide open. Here are some things to consider:

- **Know yourself.** This may take time, but as you grow into the teaching job, you will find that you enjoy teaching certain classes and students more than others. You might find you really work well with motivated upper classmen but have a difficult time motivating unruly freshmen. Or you may find that whatever the class, you gravitate to the at-risk youth. Maybe you love teaching a certain subject matter but dislike another. Sometimes, you cannot control what classes you are assigned, but if you know your strengths and weaknesses, then express them to your chairperson, and perhaps you can have some effect.
- **Choose carefully.** Choose the school system that best matches your personal criteria. Do you enjoy the rural school with small class sizes (and the same students each year), several preps, and more extracurricular activities? Or do you prefer the large-school atmosphere where you have fewer preps and larger classes (with different students each year) and are not required to take on extra duties? It may take some teaching experience to identify your criteria, but when you recognize your niche, seek it.
- **Change schools if necessary.** Do not hesitate to make a lateral move to gain a better fit in your profession. Usually, salary schedules are similar in any one geographic area. Pick the situation that suits you best, even if it means accepting a slightly lower salary.

 Golden Moment

A committed teacher explains how she managed to cope with always being assigned the low-achieving students because she was "so good with them."

Honestly, at times, it was certainly a disappointment. I often felt as if I wasn't good enough for the other classes. However, I knew better than that! Some of my fondest teaching memories come from general science and the lower level kids. The best part is the bond that I made with some of the students. I learned to laugh with them, which was a great way to connect and get them to do what I asked. Sure, there were days when I wanted to pull out my hair, but I just learned to deal with it.

I am always so very proud of my students when they are successful. Just the other day, I ran into Willie at church of all places. (You know Mr. Harley: long hair, bad attitude, boots on the table, leather, and never on time or on task.) He is now thirty-something and pursuing a degree in microbiology. He has apologized many times for being a "@#&%" in class and is glad I was able to put up with him. He told me he really did learn things and that is when his love for science began. What a proud moment.

When you feel good about where you work, and you head to class every day with a positive attitude and in good spirits, you will do the best job possible. That means your pay in "golden moments" will be on the increase. What's that you say? Golden moment currency won't pay the bills? Face it—if a high salary was your major criteria for choosing a career, you never would have become a teacher. Keep your perspective, and try for a lifelong position that you truly love.

"A gifted teacher is as rare as a gifted doctor and makes far less money." — Anonymous

You May Need Bifocal Goggles

The primary goal of every school district is to educate all of its students. The teachers are in the trenches where education truly happens. From the teachers' perspective, each day, a variety of individual student needs must be addressed to facilitate learning. A teacher's concerns with overcrowded classrooms, discipline problems, and special-needs students often seem to be ignored by administrators, who are forced to make decisions that align with state and federal guidelines within the confines of an inadequate budget. For many teachers, frustration begins when they realize they are on the lowest rung of the district hierarchy when it comes to making decisions.

Administrators view the goal of educating all students from a different perspective than the teachers. Transportation, safety, staffing, state mandates, and financial concerns are of major importance to them. It is doubtful that any school has the words "within the budget" built into its mission statement; yet, that is a driving force for decisions made within a district. This focus results in an industrial model of education where one size fits all. Class size is increased so fewer teachers are needed. Often, classroom supplies are scarce, and new textbook adoption and building repairs are delayed. At the extreme, administrators move teachers around without considering their personal attributes, sometimes forcing a square peg into a round hole.

Experienced teachers are not mourned when they leave the system; instead, the district sees an opportunity to save money. Two new teachers can be hired for the price of one experienced teacher.

Too many decisions are made due to budget constraints and then implemented with little or no respect for the feelings of the teachers involved.

 **Teacher Snapshot**

> *As a favor to her school, Danielle worked half-time as a middle-school counselor after her retirement because there were few qualified counselors available to replace her. She had been named "State Counselor of the Year" and had many innovative and successful programs in place that she was able to continue on a part-time basis. In April of her third year of this employment, the principal approached her in the hall and said they didn't need her services for the following year. Danielle didn't expect to work part-time forever, but she did expect to be appreciated and valued for her dedication to her school and to be courteously and respectfully informed that she was no longer needed.*

The variant perspectives of teachers and administrators (got those bifocal goggles?) often lead to conflict and frustration. Sometimes, it seems that the student is the last person to be considered. Hopefully, your principal listens to the staff's concerns and establishes building goals that will create a positive learning environment and maximize student progress despite the budget. A good principal includes teachers in the building decisions, empowers them, and creates good morale. Happy teachers will do their best to educate their students regardless of the conditions.

Because our educational structure changes very slowly, you must learn to survive within the existing system in your first years of teaching. Learn your craft first. Avoid getting embroiled in campus politics and taking sides on issues with which you are unfamiliar. After you have some teaching experience under your belt, then perhaps you will want to attempt to effect some change in your building or district. If you have a good administrator, change can and will happen. However, as a new teacher, you need to keep your focus on the classroom. Remember, you need to learn to swim before you attempt those complicated dives into school reform. It is imperative that you understand that the most important aspect of your job is to be a good teacher, attending to each and every one of your students. That is what really matters.

> *"A teacher's constant task is to take a roomful of live wires and see to it that they're grounded." — E. C. McKenzie.*

The Reflection Pool

Upon reflection, do you feel you are well suited to a teaching career? Why or why not?

Final Thoughts

As we shared with you earlier, the snapshots, golden moments, and stories in this book are true. The names have all been changed, and some of the snapshots are composites of students and teachers whom we have known. Soon, you will have your own collection of stories and advice to share with new teachers. Our hope is that you will enjoy your career as much as we have enjoyed ours. When you look back, we hope you will be happy and proud knowing that you have had the opportunity to make a positive difference in the lives of each of your students.

Golden Moment

In the words of an award-winning physics teacher:

Just yesterday, some students came by after school to study for a physics test. They were talking about how interesting this unit has been and how they had never thought of the many connections we made to their experiences. We were studying sound, and they were musicians. One young lady stayed afterward to tell me about her interview for a local scholarship; the interviewer had asked her to name the class in high school in which she had learned the most. She said physics, because the class had helped her to understand the wonder of nature and the awesome God who made it. That made it worth staying after school an extra hour.

As I think about the next day's lesson, I am motivated to do a good job and put

in extra time to get the demonstrations and labs prepared and repaired because I picture that student, or maybe a few students, who really want to learn. They are my boss, not some administrator who has a list of forms to fill out and rules to follow. If you build good relationships with students, you will be motivated to do a good job.

If you know and love your students and you know and love your subject, then you will find a way to teach, and they will find a way to learn. In twenty-six years of teaching science, I have never had a student go out of his/her way to come back to visit me to say "Thanks for putting those objectives on the board" or "Those scoring guides were so helpful" or "I'm glad we spent so much time on the state and national science standards." They come back to see me because of my relationship with them. They learned and had fun in my class. They felt safe and loved in my class. They want me to know they are doing well and that they love me too.

The T.Box
... Our Gift to You ... FREE!

We hope you have enjoyed our book and benefited from it. We have offered a positive, fun, down-to earth approach to teaching, which we believe to be an extremely challenging and rewarding career. The ideas and attitudes expressed are not new, but they are worth thinking about, re-defining, and applying again and again. Throughout the book you have seen references to our T.Box. This is where we offer concrete help with the application of some of the major ideas in this book. Among the downloadable resources in our T.Box you will find:

- Useful Internet sites

- Creative forms to facilitate day-to-day classroom activities

- Print-ready ideas you can implement immediately

- Fun activities to enliven the classroom and engage students

These are yours for the asking. Simply go online to our website, www.teacherstacklebox.com, and download the resources directly to your computer.

We wish you a fun, fulfilling career in education resulting in many "Golden Moments."

References

1. Berne, Eric. *Games People Play.* Random House, Inc., 1967. Harris, Thomas, M.D. *I'm OK–You're OK.* Harper & Row, 1967.
2. Coffield, F., Moseley, D., Hall, E. and Ecclestone, K. (2004) *Should we be using learning styles: What research has to say to practice.* Learning Skills Research Centre, London. http://www.ttrb.ac.uk/attachments/c455e462-95c4-4b0d-8308bbc5ed1053a7.pdf
3. Dunn, R. & Dunn, K. (1978). *Teaching Students through their individual learning styles: A practical approach.* Reston, VA: Reston Publishing Company
4. Sprenger, M. (2003). *Differentiation through learning styles and memory.* Thousand Oaks, CA: Corwin Press
5. Willmingham, D. (2005). "Do Visual, Auditory and Kinesthetic Learners Need Visual, Auditory and Kinesthetic Instruction?" *American Educator,* http://www.aft.org/newspubs/periodicals/ae/summer2005/willingham.cfm
6. Holden, J.T. (American InterContinental University); Westfall, J.L. (Air University) *Learning Styles: Implication for Instructional Design.* http://www.fgdla.us/uploads/Learning_Styles_Implications_for_Instructional_Design.pdf
7. Pashler, H., McDaniel, M., Rohrer, D., Bjork R. (2009). "Learning styles: Concepts and Evidence". *Psychological Science in the Public Interest* 9: 105-119.
8. Edgar Dale, *Audio-visual Methods in Technology,* Holt, Rinehart and Winston, 1950.
9. Rick Smith, *Conscious Classroom Management: Unlocking the Secrets of Great Teaching,* Conscious Teaching Publications, September 30, 2004, www.consciousteaching.com

10. Dicintio, M.J. and Gee, S. "Control Is the Key: Unlocking the Motivation of At-risk Students." *Psychology in the Schools* (July 1999) 231-237.
11. Lucking, R. and Manning, M.L. "Instruction for Low-achieving Young Adolescents: Addressing the Challenge of a Generation Imperiled. *Preventing School Failure* (Winter 1996) 82-87.
12. *Stress and Your Health*. womenshealth.gov.http://www.womenshealth.gov/faq/stress.htm.
13. Jaffe-Gill, Ellen, Melinda Smith, M.A., Heather Larson, and Jeanne Segal, PHD. *Understanding Stress: Signs, Symptoms, Causes, and Effects*. http://helpguide.org/mental/stress signs.htm.
14. *Stress Management: Personality and Stress*. http://health.discover.com/centers/stress/articles/pnstress/pnstress.html
15. Casey, Erin. "Habits for a Healthier Life." *Success Magazine*, August 26, 2008.
16. Smith, Melinda, M.A., Ellen Jaffe-Gill, M.A. and Robert Segal, M.A. *Stress Management: How to Reduce, Prevent and Cope with Stress*. http://helpguide.org/mental/stress_management_relief_coping_htm.
17. National Commission on Teaching and America's Future. (2003). *No dream denied: A pledge to America's children summary report*. Washington D.C.: National Commission on Teaching and America's Future.

Index

angelfish, 36
auditory learners, 58
Average Joe Fish, 82
below the waterline behaviors, 101
Bullhead, 86
cheaters, 103
clown loach, 36
commander fish, 37
Darter, 87
dealing with stress, 133
diversity, 80
Edgar Dale, 75
educational acronyms, 14
ego states, 33
eight raised hands, 84
Eric Berne, 33
Flounder, 88
Grass Carp, 90
Hatchet Fish, 94
helicopter parents, 123
I-messages, 29
invisible parents, 124
kinesthetic learners, 58
LSI's, 56
meticulo Fish, 37
motivation, 70
Nemo, 91
oppositional parents, 123
parent/teacher conference, 116
parents, 115
positive learning cycle, 70
predators, 94
reflective listening, 31
resources (downloadable), 151
Rick Smith, 84
self-efficacy, 85
signs of stress, 130
Smarty Pants Fish, 82
Solo Fish, 89
stress, 127
stress-prone personality traits, 131
T.Box, 151
T.Box: activities for classroom environment, 100
T.Box: assessment of teacher disposition, 140
T.Box: beginning activities, 51
T.Box: classroom design, 45
T.Box: discipline resources, 99
T.Box: ending activities, 52
T.Box: flowcharts foir note taking 58
T.Box: helpful forms, 122
T.Box: instead of homework cards 76

T.Box: learning
    communities, 73
T.Box: learning styles
    inventorie, 57
T.Box: lesson plan template,
    60
T.Box: MAX teaching, 77
T.Box: memory devices, 58
T. Box: sample lecture
    outlines, 87
T.Box: stress tests, 129
T.Box: trial & error activities
    59
T.Box: True Colors, 141
T-Box: ice-breaker ideas, 48
Tuned Out Fish, 83
Viper Fish, 95
visual learner, 57

Notes

Notes

Notes

Notes

Made in the USA
Lexington, KY
31 December 2018